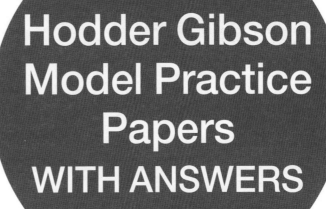

Hodder Gibson Model Practice Papers
WITH ANSWERS

PLUS: Official SQA Specimen Paper & 2014 Past Paper With Answers

National 5
Graphic Communication

2013 Specimen Question Paper,
Model Papers & 2014 Exam

Hodder Gibson Study Skills Advice – General — page 3
Hodder Gibson Study Skills Advice –
  National 5 Graphic Communication — page 5
2013 SPECIMEN QUESTION PAPER — page 7
MODEL PAPER 1 — page 33
MODEL PAPER 2 — page 53
MODEL PAPER 3 — page 71
2014 EXAM — page 95
ANSWER SECTION — page 117

HODDER GIBSON
AN HACHETTE UK COMPANY

This book contains the official 2013 SQA Specimen Question Paper and 2014 Exam for National 5 Graphic Communication, with associated SQA answers.

In addition the book contains model practice papers, together with answers, plus study skills advice. These papers, some of which may include a limited number of previously published SQA questions, have been specially commissioned by Hodder Gibson, and have been written by experienced senior teachers and examiners in line with the new National 5 syllabus and assessment outlines, Spring 2013. This is not SQA material but has been devised to provide further practice for National 5 examinations in 2014 and beyond.

Hodder Gibson is grateful to the copyright holders, as credited on the final page of the Answer Section, for permission to use their material. Every effort has been made to trace the copyright holders and to obtain their permission for the use of copyright material. Hodder Gibson will be happy to receive information allowing us to rectify any error or omission in future editions.

Hachette UK's policy is to use papers that are natural, renewable and recyclable products and made from wood grown in sustainable forests. The logging and manufacturing processes are expected to conform to the environmental regulations of the country of origin.

Orders: please contact Bookpoint Ltd, 130 Park Drive, Abingdon, Oxon OX14 4SE. Telephone: (44) 01235 827720. Fax: (44) 01235 400454. Lines are open 9.00–5.00, Monday to Saturday, with a 24-hour message answering service. Visit our website at www.hoddereducation.co.uk. Hodder Gibson can be contacted direct on: Tel: 0141 848 1609; Fax: 0141 889 6315; email: hoddergibson@hodder.co.uk

This collection first published in 2014 by
Hodder Gibson, an imprint of Hodder Education,
An Hachette UK Company
2a Christie Street
Paisley PA1 1NB

BrightRED   Hodder Gibson is grateful to Bright Red Publishing Ltd for collaborative work in preparation of this book and all SQA Past Paper, National 5 and Higher for CfE Model Paper titles 2014.

Specimen Question Paper and Answers 2013 and National 5 Exam Paper 2014 © Scottish Qualifications Authority. Model Question Papers and Answers, and Study Skills Section © Hodder Gibson. Model Question Papers creation/compilation, Answers and Study Skills section © Scott Hunter and Peter Linton. All rights reserved. Apart from any use permitted under UK copyright law, no part of this publication may be reproduced or transmitted in any form or by any means, electronic or mechanical, including photocopying and recording, or held within any information storage and retrieval system, without permission in writing from the publisher or under licence from the Copyright Licensing Agency Limited. Further details of such licences (for reprographic reproduction) may be obtained from the Copyright Licensing Agency Limited, Saffron House, 6–10 Kirby Street, London EC1N 8TS.

Typeset by PDQ Digital Media Solutions Ltd, Bungay, Suffolk NR35 1BY

Printed in the UK

A catalogue record for this title is available from the British Library

ISBN: 978-1-4718-3705-0

3 2 1

2015 2014

Introduction

Study Skills – what you need to know to pass exams!

Pause for thought

Many students might skip quickly through a page like this. After all, we all know how to revise. Do you really though?

Think about this:

"IF YOU ALWAYS DO WHAT YOU ALWAYS DO, YOU WILL ALWAYS GET WHAT YOU HAVE ALWAYS GOT."

Do you like the grades you get? Do you want to do better? If you get full marks in your assessment, then that's great! Change nothing! This section is just to help you get that little bit better than you already are.

There are two main parts to the advice on offer here. The first part highlights fairly obvious things but which are also very important. The second part makes suggestions about revision that you might not have thought about but which WILL help you.

Part 1

DOH! It's so obvious but …

Start revising in good time

Don't leave it until the last minute – this will make you panic.

Make a revision timetable that sets out work time AND play time.

Sleep and eat!

Obvious really, and very helpful. Avoid arguments or stressful things too – even games that wind you up. You need to be fit, awake and focused!

Know your place!

Make sure you know exactly **WHEN and WHERE** your exams are.

Know your enemy!

Make sure you know what to expect in the exam.

How is the paper structured?

How much time is there for each question?

What types of question are involved?

Which topics seem to come up time and time again?

Which topics are your strongest and which are your weakest?

Are all topics compulsory or are there choices?

Learn by DOING!

There is no substitute for past papers and practice papers – they are simply essential! Tackling this collection of papers and answers is exactly the right thing to be doing as your exams approach.

Part 2

People learn in different ways. Some like low light, some bright. Some like early morning, some like evening / night. Some prefer warm, some prefer cold. But everyone uses their BRAIN and the brain works when it is active. Passive learning – sitting gazing at notes – is the most INEFFICIENT way to learn anything. Below you will find tips and ideas for making your revision more effective and maybe even more enjoyable. What follows gets your brain active, and active learning works!

Activity 1 – Stop and review

Step 1

When you have done no more than 5 minutes of revision reading STOP!

Step 2

Write a heading in your own words which sums up the topic you have been revising.

Step 3

Write a summary of what you have revised in no more than two sentences. Don't fool yourself by saying, "I know it, but I cannot put it into words". That just means you don't know it well enough. If you cannot write your summary, revise that section again, knowing that you must write a summary at the end of it. Many of you will have notebooks full of blue/black ink writing. Many of the pages will not be especially attractive or memorable so try to liven them up a bit with colour as you are reviewing and rewriting. **This is a great memory aid, and memory is the most important thing.**

Activity 2 — Use technology!

Why should everything be written down? Have you thought about "mental" maps, diagrams, cartoons and colour to help you learn? And rather than write down notes, why not record your revision material?

What about having a text message revision session with friends? Keep in touch with them to find out how and what they are revising and share ideas and questions.

Why not make a video diary where you tell the camera what you are doing, what you think you have learned and what you still have to do? No one has to see or hear it, but the process of having to organise your thoughts in a formal way to explain something is a very important learning practice.

Be sure to make use of electronic files. You could begin to summarise your class notes. Your typing might be slow, but it will get faster and the typed notes will be easier to read than the scribbles in your class notes. Try to add different fonts and colours to make your work stand out. You can easily Google relevant pictures, cartoons and diagrams which you can copy and paste to make your work more attractive and **MEMORABLE**.

Activity 3 – This is it. Do this and you will know lots!

Step 1

In this task you must be very honest with yourself! Find the SQA syllabus for your subject (www.sqa.org.uk). Look at how it is broken down into main topics called MANDATORY knowledge. That means stuff you MUST know.

Step 2

BEFORE you do ANY revision on this topic, write a list of everything that you already know about the subject. It might be quite a long list but you only need to write it once. It shows you all the information that is already in your long-term memory so you know what parts you do not need to revise!

Step 3

Pick a chapter or section from your book or revision notes. Choose a fairly large section or a whole chapter to get the most out of this activity.

With a buddy, use Skype, Facetime, Twitter or any other communication you have, to play the game "If this is the answer, what is the question?". For example, if you are revising Geography and the answer you provide is "meander", your buddy would have to make up a question like "What is the word that describes a feature of a river where it flows slowly and bends often from side to side?".

Make up 10 "answers" based on the content of the chapter or section you are using. Give this to your buddy to solve while you solve theirs.

Step 4

Construct a wordsearch of at least 10 X 10 squares. You can make it as big as you like but keep it realistic. Work together with a group of friends. Many apps allow you to make wordsearch puzzles online. The words and phrases can go in any direction and phrases can be split. Your puzzle must only contain facts linked to the topic you are revising. Your task is to find 10 bits of information to hide in your puzzle, but you must not repeat information that you used in Step 3. DO NOT show where the words are. Fill up empty squares with random letters. Remember to keep a note of where your answers are hidden but do not show your friends. When you have a complete puzzle, exchange it with a friend to solve each other's puzzle.

Step 5

Now make up 10 questions (not "answers" this time) based on the same chapter used in the previous two tasks. Again, you must find NEW information that you have not yet used. Now it's getting hard to find that new information! Again, give your questions to a friend to answer.

Step 6

As you have been doing the puzzles, your brain has been actively searching for new information. Now write a NEW LIST that contains only the new information you have discovered when doing the puzzles. Your new list is the one to look at repeatedly for short bursts over the next few days. Try to remember more and more of it without looking at it. After a few days, you should be able to add words from your second list to your first list as you increase the information in your long-term memory.

FINALLY! Be inspired...

Make a list of different revision ideas and beside each one write **THINGS I HAVE** tried, **THINGS I WILL** try and **THINGS I MIGHT** try. Don't be scared of trying something new.

And remember – "FAIL TO PREPARE AND PREPARE TO FAIL!"

National 5 Graphic Communication

The course

The aims of the course are to enable you to understand how graphic communication is used every day in design, industry and society and to ensure you learn skills and techniques to create graphics to suit any number of purposes.

The types of graphics you will be able to create include:

- **preliminary** design graphics
- technical **production** drawings
- high-impact **promotional** and information graphics.

These are known as the **3 Ps**.

All of your coursework projects and exam questions are based on these types of graphics. The knowledge you need for the exam will come from the work you do during your project work in class.

How you are assessed and graded

The grade you achieve at the end of your course depends on a number of assessments.

Unit Assessment

Both units (2D Graphic Communication and 3D & Pictorial Graphic Communication) are assessed on a pass or fail basis. You must pass both units in order to qualify for a course award.

Course Assessment

Your grade for the National 5 course is derived from two course assessments:

- **The assignment:** this is the project you will complete during the second half of your course. It is worth 60 marks.
- **The course exam paper:** this is the exam you will sit at the end of the course. It is worth 60 marks.

Your marks for the two assessments are added together to give you a total out of 120 marks.

The exam

Duration: 1 hour and 30 minutes

Marks available: 60

The exam will include a mix of short and more extended response questions about the graphics required to design, produce or promote a product.

You should look at the marks awarded for each question. This is a good indicator of the length of answer you should give. For example, for a 3-mark question you will need to make three distinct points, while for a 1-mark question you will need to make only a single point. You should allow yourself around one and a half minutes per mark.

Sketching

Exam questions will be set so that you can answer in writing. However, some questions will invite you to answer using annotated sketches or drawings and space will be left so that you can sketch your answer. **Always take this opportunity.**

Remember:

- This is an exam about graphics and you have all the graphic skills you need.
- It is easier and quicker to describe your answer graphically with annotations than it is to write about it.
- The quality of sketching will not be assessed but the clarity of your answer is important. So make sure your sketches and annotations are clear.

Skills and knowledge

The exam will test you on the following skills and knowledge:

- **Problem solving:** How would you model, render or assemble a 3D CAD model?
- **Creative skills:** How has the graphic designer used design elements and principles to achieve an effective layout?
- **DTP features and edits:** How has the graphic designer used DTP (desktop publishing) software to achieve an effective layout?
- **Advantages and disadvantages:** What are the best methods to choose when creating graphics?
- **Knowledge of drawing standards:** What drawing standards should be applied to orthographic and pictorial drawings?
- **Spatial awareness:** Can you interpret and understand drawings?
- **Graphics in society:** How do graphics affect society? How do we use information graphics?
- **Graphics and the environment:** How can we create and use graphics without damaging our fragile environment?

Using this book

Practising the type of questions you are likely to face in the National 5 exam is vital if you are to achieve your highest possible grade. This book will give you experience of the problem solving and creative layout questions you will encounter in the exam.

Answering 3D CAD modelling problem solving questions

You should always:

- study the model
- identify what modelling techniques have been used (extrude or revolve)
- describe the steps: new sketch, draw profile, select axis, revolve, etc.
- include the dimensions provided
- describe any additional edits used: array, subtract, shell, etc.
- and, importantly, make annotated sketches to show the steps clearly.

Answering creative layout questions

These questions will ask you to identify how DTP features have been used in a layout and how design elements and principles have been used. Some questions will test your knowledge further by asking you to explain how the use of these features improves the layout.

You should always:

- study the layout (don't rush this!)
- identify the DTP feature(s) and design elements and principles used.
  - Think carefully about how they improve the layout: do they add contrast, create harmony, suggest depth, develop a dominant focal point, unify the layout, create emphasis, change the balance or connect or separate parts? The feature you are asked about will do one of these things. Your task is to identify what it does and explain how it does it.

At the end of the exam, don't forget to read over your answers. Read the questions again and double-check that you have answered the question that was asked. You should have plenty of time.

Good luck!

Remember that the rewards for passing National 5 Graphic Communication are well worth it! Your pass will help you get the future you want for yourself. In the exam, be confident in your own ability. If you're not sure how to answer a question, trust your instincts and just give it a go anyway. Keep calm and don't panic! GOOD LUCK!

Oh, and there is a really exciting Higher course waiting for you next year; we'll see you there!

2013 Specimen Question Paper

N5

National Qualifications
SPECIMEN ONLY

SQ21/N5/01

Graphic Communication

Date — Not applicable

Duration — 1 hour and 30 minutes

Total marks — 60

Attempt ALL questions.

All dimensions are in mm.

All technical sketches and drawings use third angle projection.

You may use rulers, compasses or trammels for measuring.

Use **blue** or **black** ink.

Before leaving the examination room you must give this booklet to the Invigilator.
If you do not, you may lose all the marks for this paper.

MARKS

1. A graphic designer has produced three promotional layouts.

(a) (i) State one instance where alignment has been used in Layout 1.

_____

_____

1

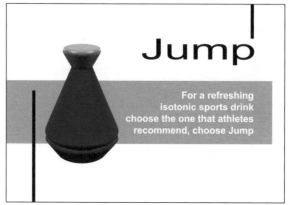

Layout 1

(ii) Describe the effect that alignment has on Layout 1.

_____

_____

_____

_____

1

(b) Describe **two** ways in which the designer has created **unity** in Layout 2.

_____

_____

_____

_____

_____

2

Layout 2

MARKS | DO NOT WRITE IN THIS MARGIN

1. **(continued)**

(c) Describe **two** methods used to create contrast in Layout 3.

Layout 3

2

_____

_____

_____

_____

_____

Early in the design process, the designer decided it was important to move the bottle away from Position 1 to Position 2 as shown below.

Position 1 **Position 2**

(d) State **one** reason for doing this.

_____

1

MARKS | DO NOT WRITE IN THIS MARGIN

1. **(continued)**

In the final DTP layout shown opposite, the designer chose **blue** for the background colour.

(e) (i) State whether blue is an advancing or receding colour.

1

_____

(ii) Describe the effect that the blue background colour has on the bottle.

1

_____

The colours used on the bottle itself are shades of red and green. The designer wishes to create a more **harmonious** colour scheme on the bottle and decides to change the red shade to another colour.

(f) State a **tertiary** colour the designer should try instead of red.

1

_____

The 'Jump' promotion will be published in a magazine and caring for the environment is important to the magazine publisher.

(g) State **two** ways in which the publisher can reduce the magazine's impact on the environment.

2

_____

_____

_____

_____

Using DTP software to produce a magazine brings many benefits to the publishing industry and its workforce.

(h) State **one** benefit that DTP has brought to the publishing industry (other than environmental benefits).

1

_____

Total marks 13

MARKS | DO NOT WRITE IN THIS MARGIN

1. (continued)

For a refreshing isotonic sports drink choose the one that athletes recommend, choose Jump.

Final layout

MARKS

2. A bracket is designed to secure one end of an extendable barrier used in cinema queues. The preliminary sketch is shown in the figure opposite. 3D modelling software was used to create a 3D model of the bracket.

The **profile** shown in Step 1 was drawn using 3D modelling software and using the sizes on the preliminary sketch. The 'extrude' command is used to make the profile in Step 1 into the 3D model shown in Step 2.

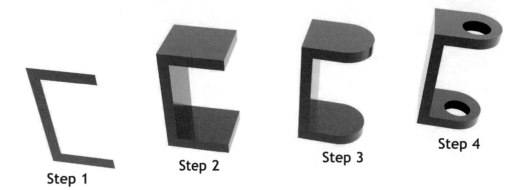

Step 1   Step 2   Step 3   Step 4

(a) State the size of the extrusion used at Step 2. _____   1

The **completed** 3D model is shown in Step 4.

(b) Describe, **with reference to correct dimensions and 3D CAD modelling terms**, how you would use 3D modelling software to complete the model from Step 3 to Step 4.   3

You may use sketches to support your answer.

_____

_____

_____

_____

_____

_____

_____

_____

_____

2. **(continued)**

Preliminary sketch of bracket

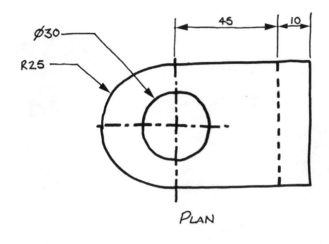

PLAN

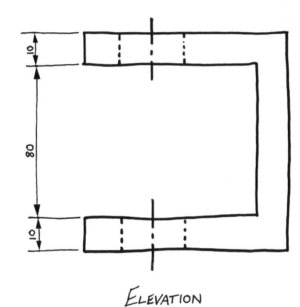

ELEVATION

MARKS | DO NOT WRITE IN THIS MARGIN

2.   (continued)

A pin is needed to secure the belt to the bracket. The pin **must not** fall through the bracket. See the figure below.

3D model of bracket

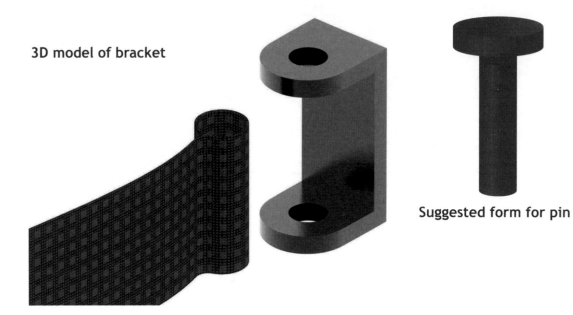

Suggested form for pin

(c) Describe, **with reference to dimensions and CAD modelling terms**, how to produce a 3D CAD model of a pin that will secure the belt to the bracket.

You must make reference to the **dimensions** on the **preliminary sketch**. A suggested form for the pin is shown above.

You may use sketches to support your answer.

4

_____

_____

_____

_____

_____

_____

_____

2.   (continued)   MARKS

An orthographic production drawing is produced from the 3D CAD model as shown below.

There are errors in the drawing.

(d) State **three** errors in the production drawing.   3

You may annotate the drawing to support your answer.

(i)   _____

(ii) _____

(iii) _____

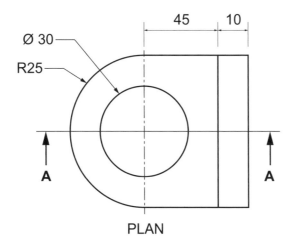

PLAN

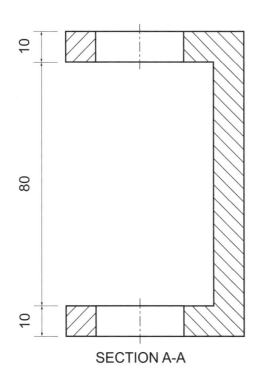

SECTION A-A

Orthographic production drawing of bracket

Total marks 11

3. Six cut geometric forms are shown as orthographic views. Options for true shapes are given opposite and contain **only six** correct true shapes which match the cut geometric forms.

Place the number of the matching true shape in the box under each cut geometric form in the orthographic views.

6

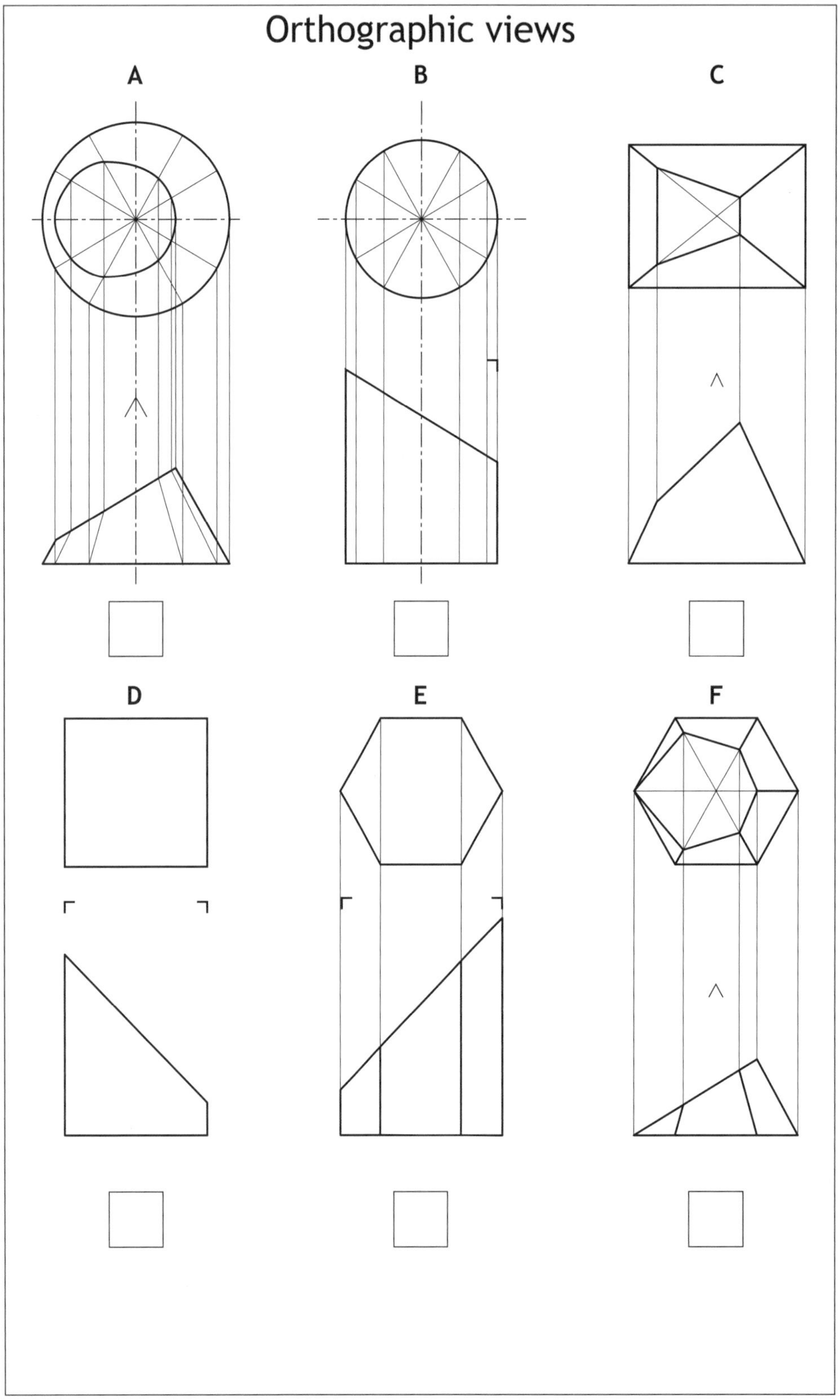

Orthographic views

A   B   C

D   E   F

MARKS

3. (continued)

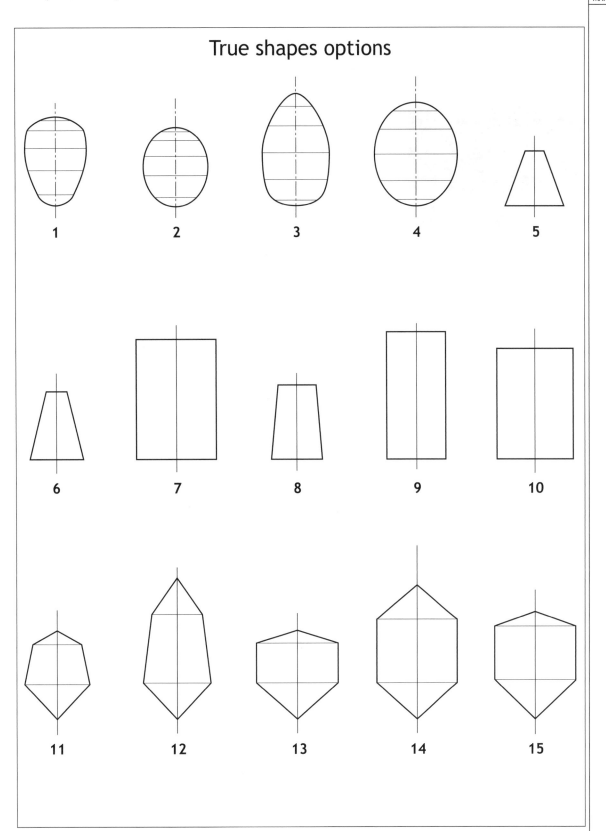

True shapes options

MARKS

4. A company that makes bicycles is celebrating a successful year. They have excellent sales figures and want to use them to help promote their success.

A graphic designer has been asked to produce graphs or charts that make the sales figures more visual for use in promotional graphics. The sales figures are shown below.

Sales figures A

Worldwide bicycle sales by percentage in 2011

UK sales	37%
European sales	27%
USA sales	20%
Australian sales	11%
Sales in other countries	5%

Sales figures B

Monthly bicycle sales in 2011

Month	Number of sales
Jan	1,600
Feb	1,100
Mar	1,200
Apr	2,600
May	2,200
Jun	3,200
Jul	5,600
Aug	6,900
Sept	2,400
Oct	1,150
Nov	1,100
Dec	9,250

(a) Based on Sales figures A:

(i) state the best type of graph or chart to use when presenting **Sales figures A** information.   1

_____

(ii) state one reason for using this type of graph or chart.   1

_____

(b) Based on Sales figures B:

(i) state the best type of graph or chart to show the **Sales figures B** over the year.   1

_____

(ii) state one reason for using this type of graph or chart.   1

_____

Total marks   4

5. (a) A floor plan with some electrical symbols is shown below.

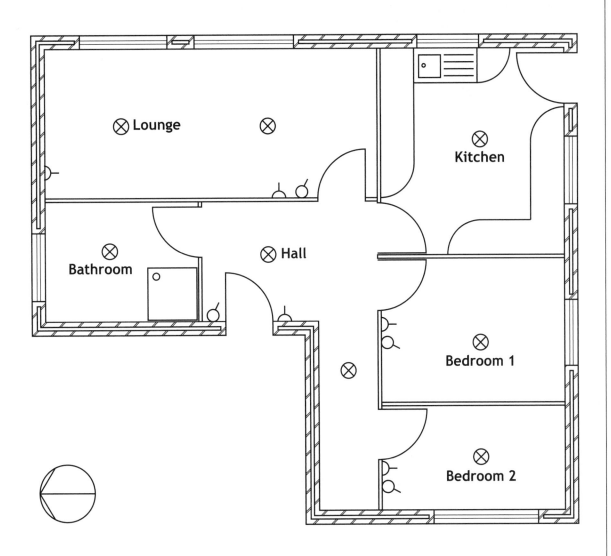

Floor plan

(continued overleaf)

MARKS | DO NOT WRITE IN THIS MARGIN

5.   (a)   (continued)

     (i)   Identify, by placing an X in the appropriate box, which symbol represents a light switch.   1

     (ii)   How many windows face east?   1

_____

(b)   All of the symbols shown above are stored in a CAD library.

     (i)   State **one** advantage of using a CAD library.   1

_____

     (ii)   State **one** advantage of using symbols in graphic communication.   1

_____

Total marks   4

MARKS | DO NOT WRITE IN THIS MARGIN

6. Orthographic CAD drawings for a new door handle assembly are shown below.

Pictorial views 1 to 5 are given on *Page seventeen*.

(a) State which pictorial view matches the door handle in the orthographic production assembly drawings.　1

_____

Sectional views 6 to 9 are given on *Page seventeen*.

(b) State the correct sectional view for section A–A on the orthographic views.　1

_____

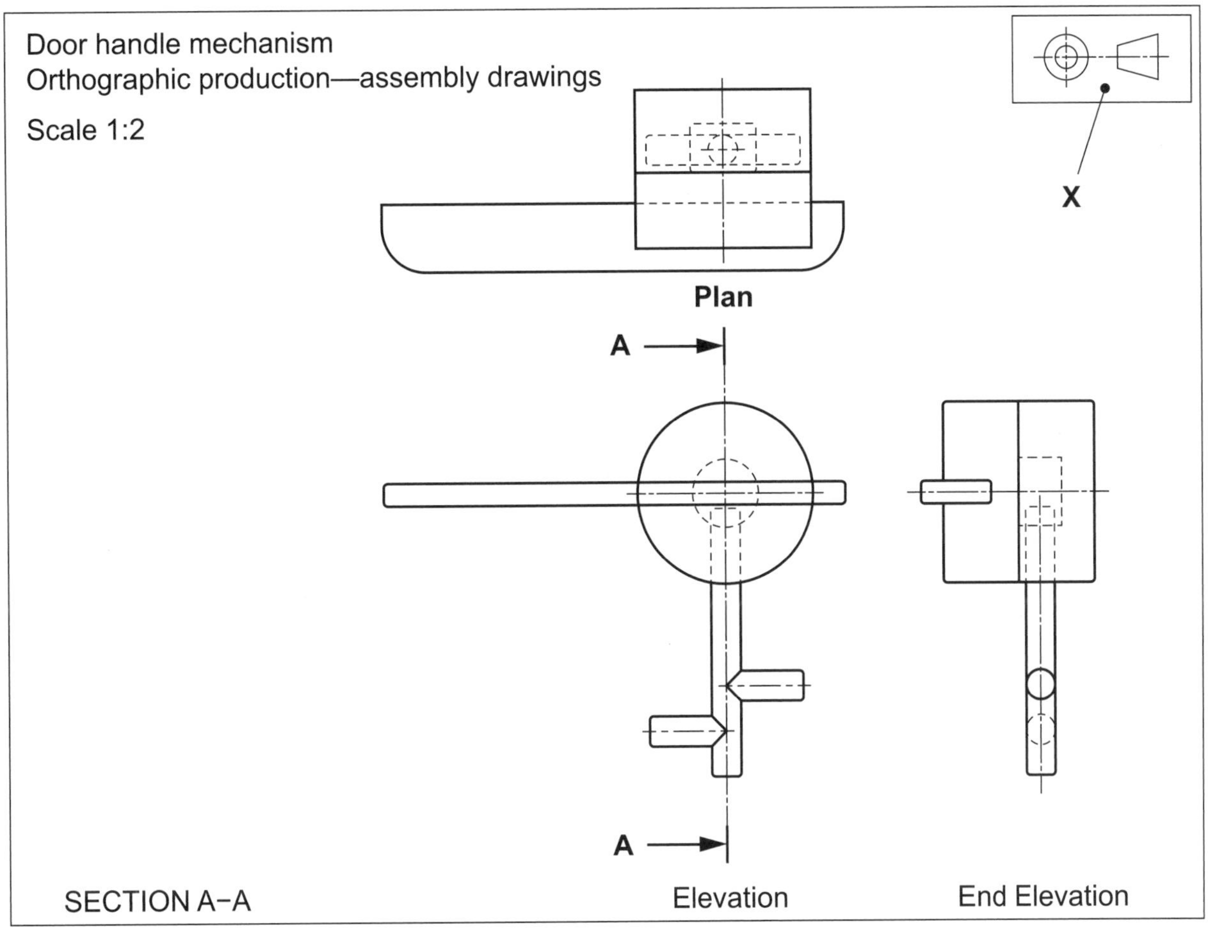

Door handle mechanism
Orthographic production—assembly drawings

Scale 1:2

Plan

X

A →

A →

SECTION A–A　　　　Elevation　　　End Elevation

(c) Explain what scale 1:2 means.　1

_____

MARKS | DO NOT WRITE IN THIS MARGIN

6.   (continued)

Dimensions are **not** normally added to orthographic **assembly** drawings.

(d)   State the type of orthographic production drawings that will normally include dimensions.

1

Sectional drawings are shown opposite.

(e)   State **one** benefit of using a sectional drawing in relation to this door handle.

1

(f)   State the name of the symbol shown at X.

1

(g)   Describe the purpose of the symbol shown at X.

1

(h)   State where, on orthographic drawings, the information 'All sizes in mm' would be found.

1

Total marks   8

MARKS | DO NOT WRITE IN THIS MARGIN

6. (continued)

Pictorial views

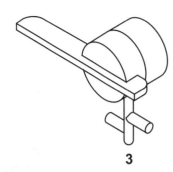
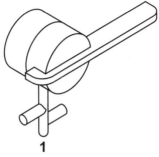
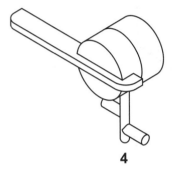
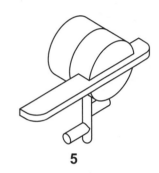

1

2

3

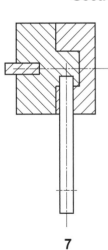
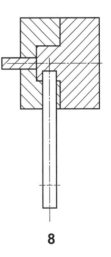
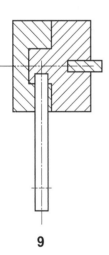

4

5

Sectional views

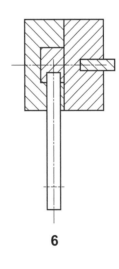

6

7

8

9

7. An outdoor supplies company is designing a range of tents for young people to take to music festivals. One of their designers has made preliminary pictorial and orthographic sketches for a possible new tent as shown below.

Preliminary pictorial sketch of festival tent

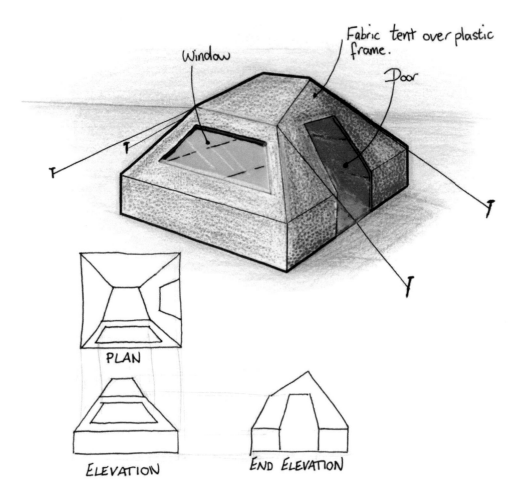

Preliminary orthographic sketch of festival tent

7. (continued)

The tent fabric is made from a single sheet. A surface development showing the **outer surface** of the tent fabric is shown below.

(a) Indicate on the surface development below, the location of:

   (i) the window—using the letter '**W**'.   1

   (ii) the door—using the letter '**D**'.   1

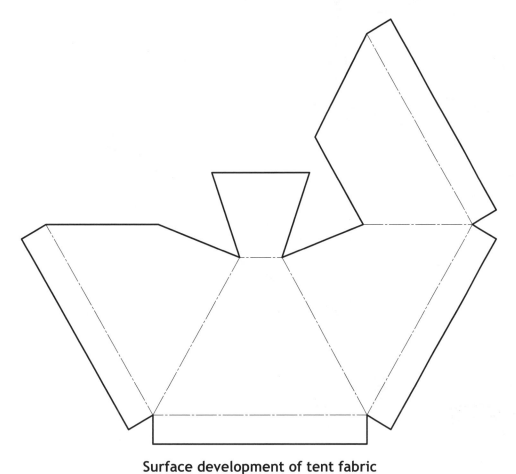

Surface development of tent fabric

MARKS | DO NOT WRITE IN THIS MARGIN

7.   (continued)

A plastic frame is used to support the tent fabric.

The frame is made from tubing and connecting brackets.

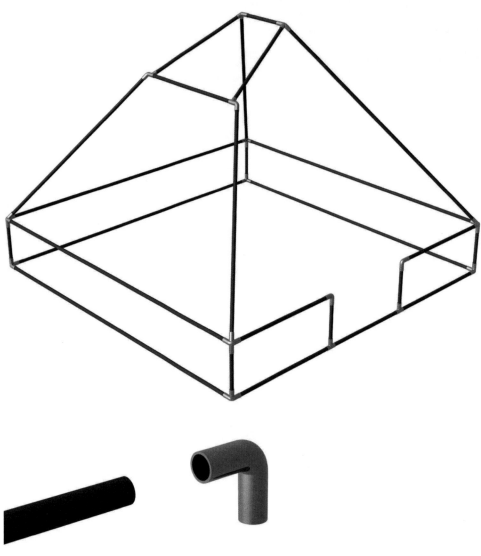

Connecting bracket and tubing for frame

MARKS

7. (continued)

An incomplete parts list of brackets has been provided below.

(b) State, in the table below, the quantity of each type of connecting bracket required to assemble the frame.

4

Part	Quantity		Part	Quantity
Bracket 1	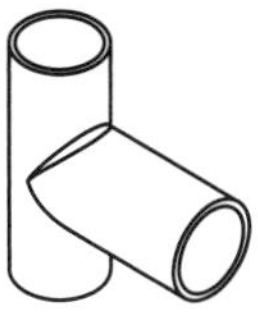 _____		Bracket 5	 1
Bracket 2	 _____		Bracket 6	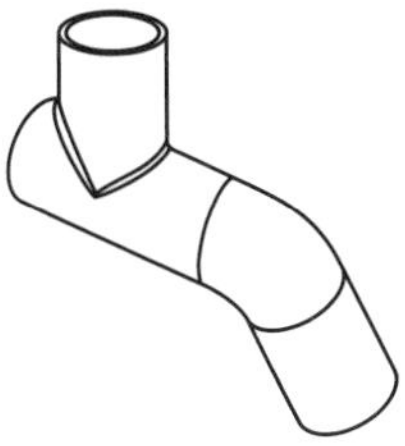 1
Bracket 3	 _____		Bracket 7	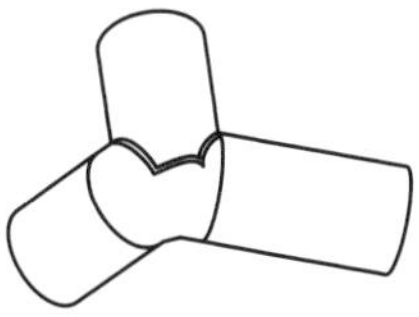 1
Bracket 4	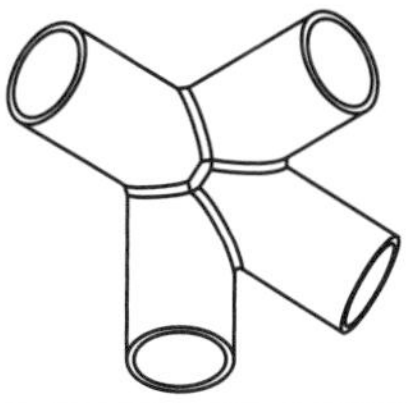 _____		Bracket 8	 1

Total Marks 6

MARKS | DO NOT WRITE IN THIS MARGIN

8. A poster promoting 'Clara', a women's perfume, is shown on the facing page.

The text and the images used in the poster are laid out in their original form at the top of the page.

The final poster layout (bottom of the page) promotes the perfume.

The original graphics and text were edited in a DTP package before being placed in the final layout.

(a) State the name of the DTP editing feature applied to each of the original items to get them ready for use in the final layout.

Do not include '**scaling** or **resizing**' in your answer.

Ensure you do not use the same answer twice.

(i) **Photograph of the model**—state **one** DTP edit.   1

Edit _____

(ii) **Perfume bottle**—state **one** DTP edit.   1

Edit _____

(iii) **'Clara' product name**—state **one** DTP edit.   1

Edit _____

(iv) **Slogan**—state **one** DTP edit (do not repeat a previous answer).   1

Edit _____

(v) **Flashbar**—state **one** DTP edit.   1

Edit _____

(b) State **one** way in which the final layout of the slogan improves the promotional poster.   1

_____

_____

(c) When setting up the layout the designer used the following DTP features: **Grid** and **Snap to grid.**

State **two** ways in which the use of **Grid** and **Snap to grid** benefit the graphic designer.   2

_____

_____

Total marks   8

8. (continued)

Text and images for final layout

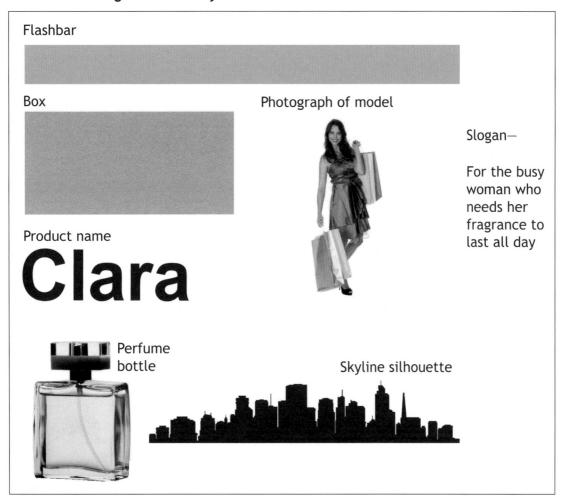

Flashbar

Box

Photograph of model

Slogan—

For the busy woman who needs her fragrance to last all day

Product name

Clara

Perfume bottle

Skyline silhouette

Final layout

[END OF SPECIMEN QUESTION PAPER]

Model Paper 1

Whilst this Model Practice Paper has been specially commissioned by Hodder Gibson for use as practice for the National 5 exams, the key reference documents remain the SQA Specimen Paper 2013 and the SQA Past Paper 2014.

National Qualifications
MODEL PAPER 1

Graphic Communication

Duration — 1 hour and 30 minutes

Total marks — 60

Attempt ALL questions.

All dimensions are in mm.

All technical sketches and drawings use third angle projection.

You may use rulers, compasses or trammels for measuring.

Use **blue** or **black** ink.

Before leaving the examination room you must give this booklet to the Invigilator.
If you do not, you may lose all the marks for this paper.

1. Cheetah Dynamics, a sports equipment company, is marketing a new range of sports shoes. The mini-ad they have produced will be used in sports magazines. The colours in the layout were chosen carefully. The red company name stands out well.

(a) State why using the colour red helps the company name to stand out against the blue and white background.   **1**

_____

_____

The designer wanted to create unity by making connections between different items in the layout.

(b) State the DTP feature that allows the body text to follow the shape of the sprinter.   **1**

_____

When line is used in a layout it can have several functions.

(c) Explain the function of the lines in this layout.   **1**

_____

_____

MARKS DO NOT WRITE IN THIS MARGIN

1. (continued)

(d) State the name of the DTP feature that produced the **waves in the slogan** above the sports shoes. **1**

___

(e) State the name of the other DTP feature used on the **wavy text**. **1**

___

(f) Explain how shaping the wavy text in this way improves the layout. **1**

___

___

The blue background **colour fill** was created by the designer.

(g) State the name of the fill effect used in the blue background. **1**

___

Total marks 7

MARKS | DO NOT WRITE IN THIS MARGIN

2. A furniture designer has created some preliminary sketches for a new chair. These sketches were given to a CAD technician who will make a 3D CAD model.

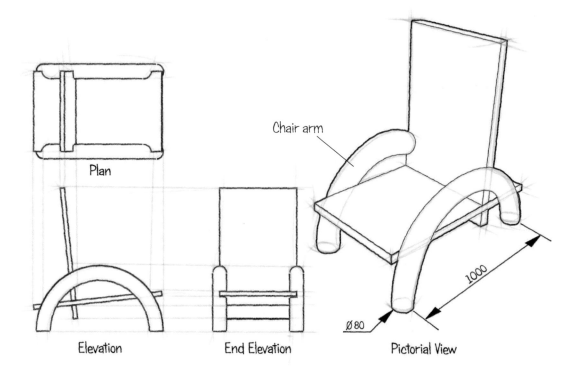

Chair arm

Plan

Elevation   End Elevation   Pictorial View

Ø 80   1000

The CAD technician used the revolve command to model the arms of the chair.

(a) Describe, **using the correct dimensions and 3D CAD modelling terms**, how you would use 3D CAD software to model one arm of the chair. **Do not model the slots in the arm.** You may use sketches to support your answer.

3

_____

_____

_____

2. **(continued)**

The chair requires two arms – one for the left and one for the right. The CAD technician modelled the left-hand arm first.

(b) Describe how the CAD technician can make an identical right-hand arm without starting a new model.

2

_____

_____

_____

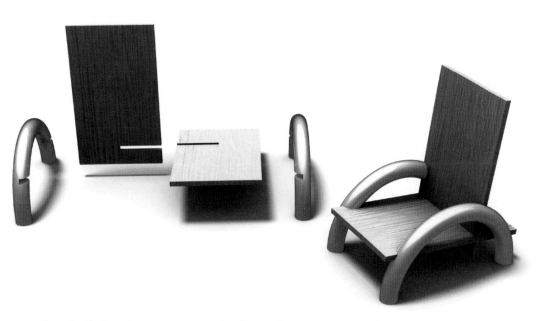

The chair has four parts, made from three components:

- the left-hand arm
- the right-hand arm
- the seat/back component (used twice).

(continued overleaf)

MARKS | DO NOT WRITE IN THIS MARGIN

2. (continued)

(c) Describe the CAD constraints used to make a CAD assembly of the four parts. Use sketches to illustrate your answer.   4

_____

_____

_____

_____

_____

Total marks   9

3. CAD production drawings for the manufacture of a plastic fixing clip are shown below.

    The drawings were to be produced in accordance with British Standards conventions but they are not correct.

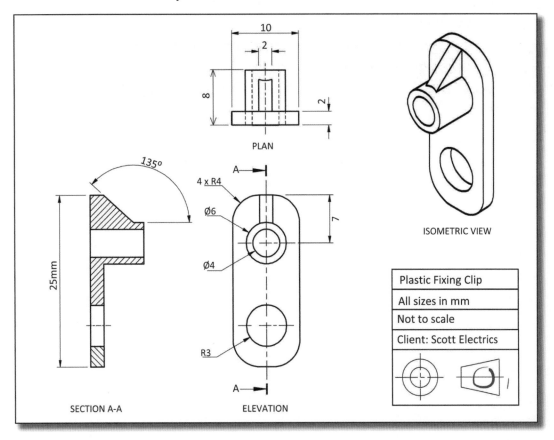

    To enable the manufacture of the clip, the production drawings require one more dimension, dimension 'X'.

    (a) Identify this missing dimension and add it to an orthographic view. There is no need to add the size, just show the leader and dimension lines and put an 'X' in place of the size. Apply the correct drawing standards. **2**

MARKS

3. (continued)

(b) Identify eight British Standards drawing **errors** or **omissions** on the orthographic production drawings on *Page seven*. Circle and number each error on the drawing and describe each error in the table below. An example has been given.

8

Table of British Standards errors and omissions in the fixing clip production drawing	
Your numbered error or omission	Description of error or omission
1	This should be a centre line, not a solid line.

The clip drawings were produced using 3D CAD modelling software. The plastic clip will be used inside a flatscreen TV which is being designed and assembled in Scotland.

All of the components are made in a factory in China before being shipped over to Scotland.

(c) Describe two ways in which **CAD models** and **drawing standards** can make this **international work** easier.

CAD Models:

1

_____

_____

Drawing Standards:

1

_____

_____

3.   (continued)

The company is always trying to improve component design. To help their designers they are transferring all of their drawings and design work from manual drawing boards to 3D CAD models.

(d) Explain two ways in which this change will benefit the designer.   2

_____

_____

The plastic clip is assembled with two other components. The drawings below show the orthographic exploded views of all three components.

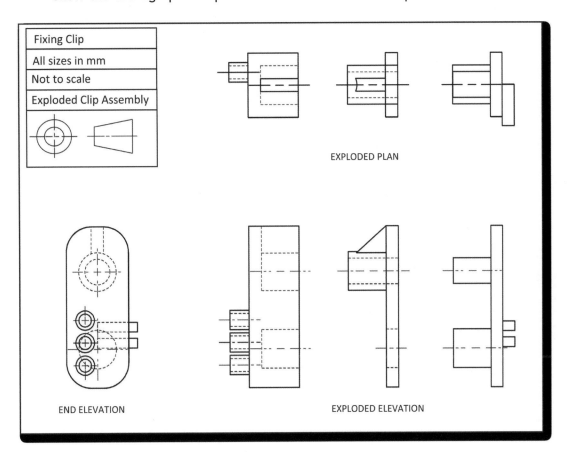

(continued overleaf)

MARKS | DO NOT WRITE IN THIS MARGIN

3. **(continued)**

The exploded pictorial drawings below represent the clip assembly.

Five of them are incorrect and one is correct.

(e) Identify the exploded pictorial view that matches the clip assembly on the previous page.

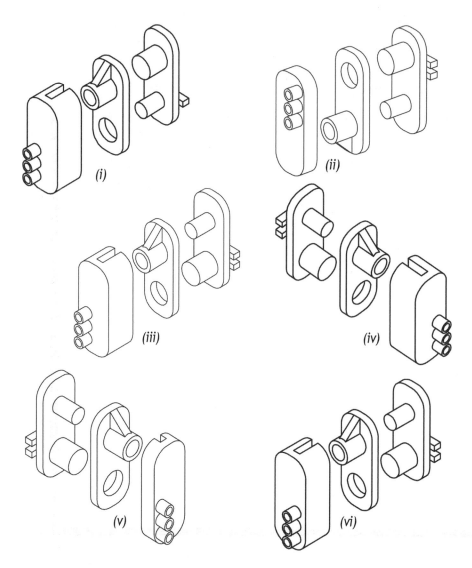

Exploded pictorial view _____ matches the clip assembly on the previous page.

1

Total marks   15

MARKS

4. A hospital has employed a graphic designer to improve the layout of signs and notices for patients.

The original sign and the improved sign are shown below.

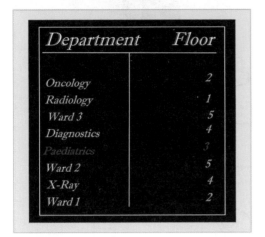

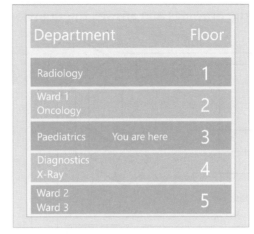

Original sign   **Improved sign**

Colour was an important consideration when designing the improved sign.

(a) Explain how the new colours improved the sign.   2

_____

_____

_____

A survey of patients and visitors preferred the choice of typeface (font) in the improved sign.

(b) Suggest a reason why the new typeface was preferred.   1

_____

_____

Visitors felt that it was easier and quicker to understand the improved sign.

(c) Identify two layout features, excluding typeface, that make the improved sign quicker to understand.   2

_____

_____

_____

Total marks   5

5. A range of production drawings for a domestic wall hook are shown. The hook comprises two components, the hook and the wall bracket, plus a standard component fixing screw.

Study the drawings and answer the questions.

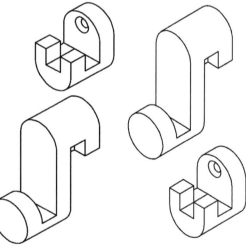

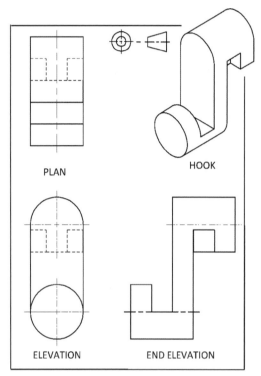

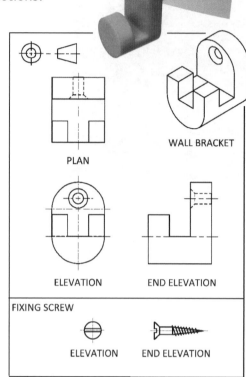

(a) State which of the two isometric exploded views is **incorrectly** exploded.

Isometric exploded view _____ is incorrectly exploded.   1

(b) Explain why this view is **incorrectly** exploded.   1

_____

_____

_____

_____

The fixing screw is missing from the exploded views.

VIEW A   **VIEW B**

Isometric exploded views

(c) Indicate the position and direction of the fixing screw on the correctly exploded isometric view.   1

MARKS

5. (continued)

Wall hook assembly drawings

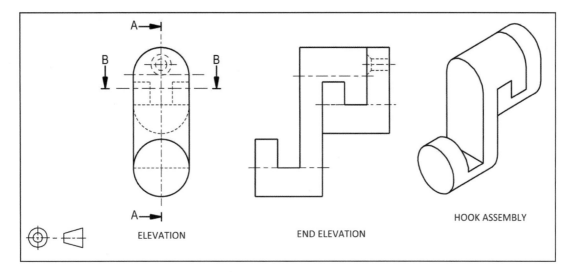

ELEVATION   END ELEVATION   HOOK ASSEMBLY

(d) Identify the sectional view below that matches section A–A above.

Section A–A is view _____.   1

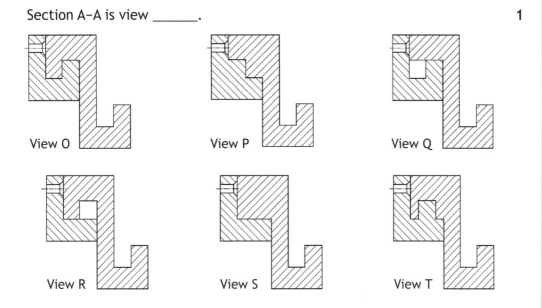

View O   View P   View Q

View R   View S   View T

(e) Identify the sectional plan view below that matches section B–B above.

Section B–B is view _____.   1

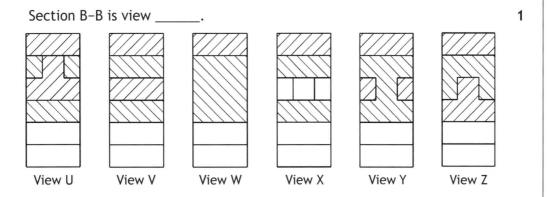

View U   View V   View W   View X   View Y   View Z

MARKS | DO NOT WRITE IN THIS MARGIN

5. **(continued)**

Exploded views and sectional views are commonly used in production drawings.

(f) Describe one benefit that **exploded views** provide.   **1**

_____

_____

(g) Describe one benefit that **sectional views** provide. Do not repeat an answer from (f).   **1**

_____

_____

In sectional drawings there are features that should not be sectioned or cross-hatched.

(h) Name one common feature or component that should **not** be sectioned.   **1**

_____

Production drawings can be shown in two main types: assembly drawings and component drawings.

(i) Describe the difference between assembly drawings and component drawings.   **1**

_____

_____

Component drawings are dimensioned to support manufacture.

(j) State why dimensions are added to component drawings and not to assembly drawings.   **1**

_____

_____

Total marks 10

MARKS | DO NOT WRITE IN THIS MARGIN

6. The four main types of information graphs and charts are shown below.

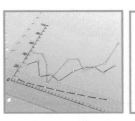

Average Holiday Prices (in £)			
	Britain	Europe	America
Spring	1800	1600	2100
Summer	2200	2000	2400
Autumn	1700	1600	1900
Winter	1350	1300	1650

| **Pie chart** | **Bar graph** | **Line graph** | **Table** |

Two different sets of statistics are shown below.

Each of the statistics can be made more visual by creating an information graph or chart to display the figures.

Statistics A
Annual ice cream sales

January	950 ltr
February	800 ltr
March	1250 ltr
April	3100 ltr
May	2750 ltr
June	4500 ltr
July	5600 ltr
August	6200 ltr
September	4210 ltr
October	1220 ltr
November	1000 ltr
December	1400 ltr

Statistics B
Road bike technical data
Model

Roadster Wheel size **590cm** Frame size **147cm** Gears **9** Weight **13kg**

Flyer Wheel size **602cm** Frame size **152cm** Gears **12** Weight **12kg**

Kingfisher Wheel size **600cm** Frame size **155cm** Gears **9** Weight **14kg**

Draper Wheel size **588cm** Frame size **148cm** Gears **8** Weight **14kg**

XRB Wheel size **640cm** Frame size **160cm** Gears **10** Weight **12kg**

Speedster Wheel size **580cm** Frame size **154cm** Gears **9** Weight **15kg**

(a) State the best type of information graphic to show the trends over the year in **Statistics A**.   1

_____

(b) Explain why this is the best type of graph or chart to display **Statistics A**.   1

_____

_____

(c) State the best type of information graphic to display the data in **Statistics B**.   1

_____

(d) Explain why this is the best type of graph or chart to display **Statistics B**.   1

_____

_____

Total marks   4

7. An architecture company makes use of preliminary, production and promotional graphics.

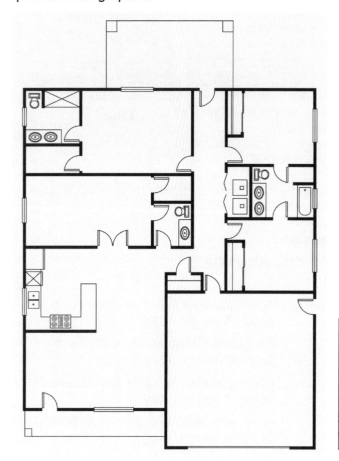

FLOOR PLAN v1.0	
HOUSE NAME:	THE ROCKWELL
SCALE:	
UNITS ARE IN M	
IF IN DOUBT, ASK!	
DRAWN BY:	CLARE HALLIDAY
APPROVED BY:	JOE MASON
DATE:	8TH JULY

To enable the builder to start constructing the house, more information needs to be added to the floor plan.

(a) State three key items of information missing from the floor plan.   3

_____

_____

_____

(b) Add the symbol for a radiator to any one of the rooms.   1

Total marks   4

MARKS

8. A poster designed by a graphic artist to encourage young people to consider university courses is shown.

(a) Describe how the graphic artist created unity in the layout.   1

_____

_____

(b) Describe how the graphic artist created depth in the layout.   1

_____

_____

The graphic artist worked hard to design an organised layout. This was achieved by using alignment.

(c) Describe where alignment occurs in the layout.   1

_____

_____

The designer used colour to create contrast in the layout.

(d) Describe one other way in which contrast has been created in this layout.   1

_____

_____

The layout is to be used on the side of double-decker buses in towns around the country.

(e) Explain why contrast is important in a promotional layout like this one.   1

_____

_____

MARKS

8. **(continued)**

(f) Choose the most dominant item in the layout and explain how the designer made it the most dominant item.

1

The most dominant item is_____

The designer created dominance by_____

_____

_____

Total marks   6

[END OF MODEL PRACTICE PAPER]

Model Paper 2

Whilst this Model Practice Paper has been specially commissioned by Hodder Gibson for use as practice for the National 5 exams, the key reference documents remain the SQA Specimen Paper 2013 and the SQA Past Paper 2014.

National Qualifications
MODEL PAPER 2

Graphic Communication

Duration — 1 hour and 30 minutes

Total marks — 60

Attempt ALL questions.

All dimensions are in mm.

All technical sketches and drawings use third angle projection.

You may use rulers, compasses or trammels for measuring.

Use **blue** or **black** ink.

Before leaving the examination room you must give this booklet to the Invigilator.
If you do not, you may lose all the marks for this paper.

HODDER GIBSON
LEARN MORE

1. Zeus Electronics are promoting their new communicator, the L-COM. Their promotions team have drawn up two promotional layouts for consideration, shown below.

L-COM Promotional layout 1

L-COM Promotional layout 2

Layout 1 was produced first. DTP edits were then made to some of the items to create layout 2.

(a) State the names of the DTP edits used to change the following items between layout 1 and layout 2.

4

The L-COM product name

DTP edit _____

The slogan ('A NEW DAWN ...' etc.)

DTP edit _____

The body text

DTP edit _____

The image of the L-COM product

DTP edit _____

MARKS | DO NOT WRITE IN THIS MARGIN

1. **(continued)**

It is important to create unity in a layout in order to hold the layout together and improve visual impact.

(b) Describe two ways in which the graphic designer has created unity in layout 2.

2

_____

_____

_____

In both layouts the product image of the L-COM communicator is the dominant item in the layout.

(c) Explain two things the graphic designer has done to make the product image the dominant item.

2

_____

_____

_____

The graphic designer felt it was important to include eye-catching contrast in the layouts. One way he achieved this was through the use of colour.

(d) State two **other ways** in which the graphic designer has created contrast in the layouts.

2

_____

_____

_____

The yellow and orange flash-bar behind the layout has been changed in layout 2 to create a style of balance that offers more visual impact.

(e) State the style of balance achieved by the change.

1

_____

MARKS DO NOT WRITE IN THIS MARGIN

1. **(continued)**

The red line in layout 2 is carefully chosen and positioned to enhance the layout.

(f) Describe one way in which the red line benefits layout 2 (do not repeat a previous answer).   1

_____

_____

The web address and the 'World Electronics' text are placed in the spaces at the top and bottom of the layouts.

(g) State the names given to these spaces in a layout.   2

Space at the top _____

Space at the bottom _____

(h) State the name of the DTP feature applied to the web address in layout 1.   1

_____

Total marks 15

2. A furniture company wants to expand its range of desk lights and has employed a design engineer to create a new flat-pack version. The design engineer used 3D CAD to illustrate her proposal.

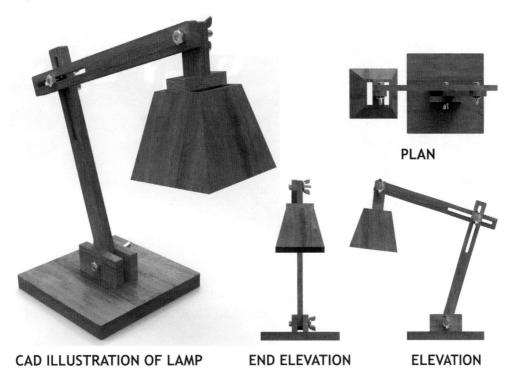

PLAN

CAD ILLUSTRATION OF LAMP   **END ELEVATION**   **ELEVATION**

The design engineer used the extrude command to make the base of the lamp. The base of the lamp requires two rectangular holes, identical in size and accurately centred on the base, to allow the vertical components to fit in.

An incomplete profile with one rectangle correctly in place is shown below.

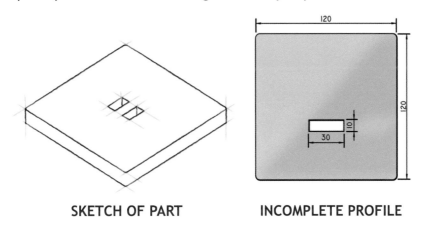

SKETCH OF PART   **INCOMPLETE PROFILE**

(a) Describe how the second hole can be drawn on the incomplete profile using only the information shown here. You may sketch directly onto the incomplete profile to help explain your answer.

2

_____

_____

_____

2. (continued)

A range of CAD components are illustrated below.

(b) Describe, **using 3D CAD terms**, how you would assemble and constrain the components above. You may use sketches to illustrate your answer. **4**

_____

_____

_____

_____

MARKS | DO NOT WRITE IN THIS MARGIN

2. (continued)

The bolt and the wing-nut were loaded from a 3D CAD library of standard components.

(c) Describe two benefits of a CAD library of standard components.   **2**

_____

_____

_____

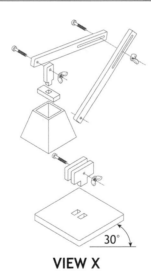

30°

VIEW X

(d) Identify the type of pictorial view shown at view X.   **1**

_____

(e) Explain how view X can be used to support a customer.   **1**

_____

_____

MARKS

2. (continued)

Two illustrated versions of the lamp are shown below.

The design engineer illustrated the 3D CAD model by applying different materials. This tested the appearance of the lamp in different materials and colours.

(f) Describe two other ways the 3D CAD model can be used to test the design of the lamp.

2

_____

_____

_____

Total marks 12

3. Images and orthographic production drawings of a new candle holder are shown opposite. It is being marketed as the OVO Candle Holder.

The OVO Candle Holder is a single component and has a second component, the mirror, added. It is not sold with the tea-light candle and the drawings below do **not** include a tea-light candle.

3. (continued)

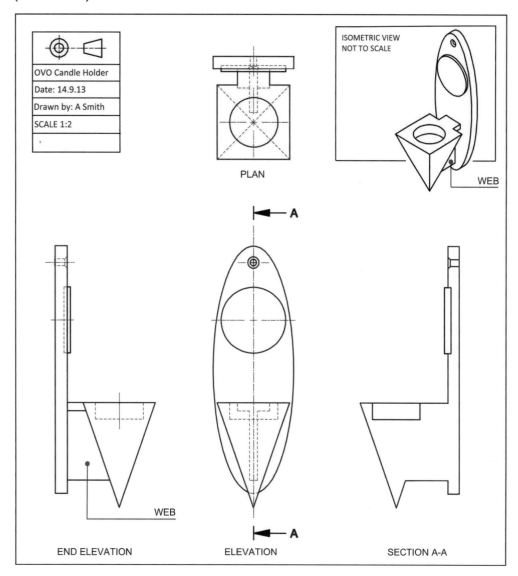

The view of section A–A is incomplete.

(a) Complete the view of section A-A by applying British Standards conventions and adding relevant features. You should sketch or draw the missing features directly onto the incomplete section A–A or you may annotate section A–A to describe your answer.

7

MARKS

3. **(continued)**

The orthographic production drawings are to be dimensioned to support manufacture.

(b) Add three dimensions, of the types listed below, to the orthographic views on the previous page.

Measure three suitable sizes on the drawings before adding the dimensions, correctly applying British Standards conventions, including scale.

- One length 2

- One breadth 2

- One diameter 2

The end elevation shown below is to have the mirror and tea-light candle added in an orthographic exploded view.

(d) Indicate suitable positions for the mirror and the tea-light candle in the exploded end elevation below. You may sketch or draw your answer or annotate the drawing to explain your answer. 2

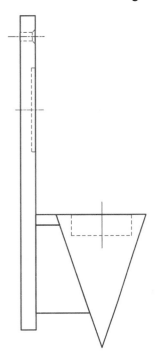

EXPLODED END ELEVATION

Total marks 15

4. A company who specialise in scale model construction kits and wooden toys have produced two promotional adverts. The adverts will be used to promote the company to different target markets.

The first advert is aimed at a **target market** comprising:

Gender	Male and female
Age	8–12 years and their parents
Interests	Toys and creative play
TV influences	Cartoons and children's programmes

The second advert focuses on a **target market** comprising:

Gender	Male
Age	35–65 years
Interests	Crafts and modelling
TV influences	Home improvement shows

Advert 1

Advert 2

MARKS

DO NOT WRITE IN THIS MARGIN

4. **(continued)**

Advert 1 makes use of the colour red in the company name.

(a) State whether red is an advancing or a receding colour.   1

_____

(b) Describe the effect this colour has on the title in the layout of advert 1.   1

_____

_____

(c) Explain why the colours used in the layout of advert 2 were chosen.   1

_____

_____

The two adverts use very different font styles in the **company name**.

With reference to the font styles:

(d) Explain why the different fonts are considered suitable for each advert.

   Advert 1: Font Style Kristen ITC   1

_____

_____

   Advert 2: Font style Batang   1

_____

_____

The company chose not to print their promotional adverts. Instead, they sent them to potential customers using email.

(e) Describe one advantage and one disadvantage of this marketing approach.

   Advantage _____   1

   Disadvantage _____   1

Total marks   7

MARKS | DO NOT WRITE IN THIS MARGIN

5. A new set of headphones have been released by SND1.

To promote their new headphones, SND1 have employed a graphic designer to create a new display stand. The display stand will be made from sheet metal.

3D CAD illustrations and orthographic views of the design are shown below.

PLAN

ELEVATION

END ELEVATION

ILLUSTRATED PICTORIAL VIEW

The graphic designer chose to make a 3D CAD model rather than a full-size card prototype of the display stand.

(a) Give two reasons why a 3D CAD model was more suitable than the card prototype. 2

_____

_____

_____

The graphic designer gave the illustration to a CAD engineer, including key information about the display stand. One piece of information stated: **A/C 400mm.**

(b) Explain the term 'A/C' and how it is used to draw this product. 2

_____

_____

_____

MARKS

5. (continued)

The graphic designer initially only made the illustrated pictorial view of the stand. The CAD engineer created the orthographic views shown below.

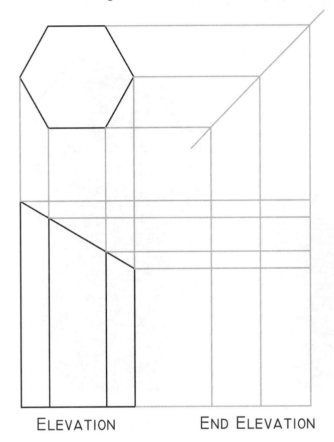

ELEVATION   END ELEVATION

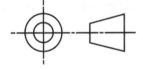

(c) Give two reasons why the CAD engineer would produce orthographic views of the display stand.

2

_____

_____

_____

_____

(d) Complete the end elevation shown above by plotting the edges on the surface generators. You may sketch or draw lines or plot corner points. Do not include hidden detail.

4

MARKS

5. (continued)

The graphic designer used 2D CAD software to generate the true shape of the sloping face of the hexagonal prism.

(e) Identify the correct true shape by ticking a box below.

1

Total marks 11

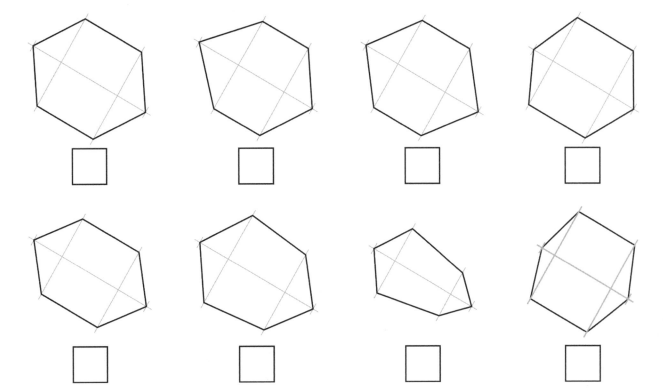

[END OF MODEL PRACTICE PAPER]

Model Paper 3

Whilst this Model Practice Paper has been specially commissioned by Hodder Gibson for use as practice for the National 5 exams, the key reference documents remain the SQA Specimen Paper 2013 and the SQA Past Paper 2014.

National Qualifications MODEL PAPER 3

Graphic Communication

Duration — 1 hour and 30 minutes

Total marks — 60

Attempt ALL questions.

All dimensions are in mm.

All technical sketches and drawings use third angle projection.

You may use rulers, compasses or trammels for measuring.

Use **blue** or **black** ink.

Before leaving the examination room you must give this booklet to the Invigilator.
If you do not, you may lose all the marks for this paper.

MARKS

1.

Final promotional layout for 'Refresh' isotonic sports drink

Colour Fill

Jogger

Slogan

When you break through the pain barrier you need the drink to refresh your body, sooth the mind and ease your thirst

Product name

Refresh

Original graphic items before editing for use in promotional layout

MARKS | DO NOT WRITE IN THIS MARGIN

1. **(continued)**

Shown at the top of the previous page is a promotional layout for a new soft drink called 'Refresh'. Some of the original graphic items used in the layout are shown at the bottom of the previous page.

Note: Do not refer to **resizing** in any of your answers and **do not repeat** your answers.

(a) State the name of the **DTP edit** used to prepare the **colour fill** for use in the final layout.   1

_____

(b) State the name of the **DTP edit** used to prepare the **slogan** for the final layout.   1

_____

(c) State the full name of the **DTP edit** used to prepare the **jogger** image for the final layout.   1

_____

(d) Describe how the DTP edit from part (c) **benefits** the layout.   1

_____

_____

(e) State the name of **one DTP edit** used to prepare the **product name** for use in the layout.   1

_____

The web address is located in the space at the bottom of the page.

(f) State what this space is called.   1

_____

Alignment has been used in the final promotional layout.

(g) State exactly **where** alignment is used in the final layout.   1

_____

MARKS

1. **(continued)**

(h) State how the use of alignment **benefits** the layout.   1

_____

_____

(i) Describe **two** different ways in which the graphic designer has created **unity** in the layout.   2

_____

_____

_____

_____

(j) Describe how the graphic designer has created **depth** in the layout.   1

_____

_____

(k) Explain how the graphic designer has made the bottle the most **dominant** item in the layout.   1

_____

_____

The **colour matching** or **colour picker** tool (also called the eye-dropper tool) was used in the creation of the 'Refresh' layout.

(l) Explain the benefit of this tool in creating the 'Refresh' layout.   1

_____

_____

Total marks 13

2. A product design engineer has sketched an idea for a simple egg cup and given this to a CAD technician for them to create a 3D CAD model.

The elevation and plan of the egg cup body, along with a sketch of the completed egg cup are shown below.

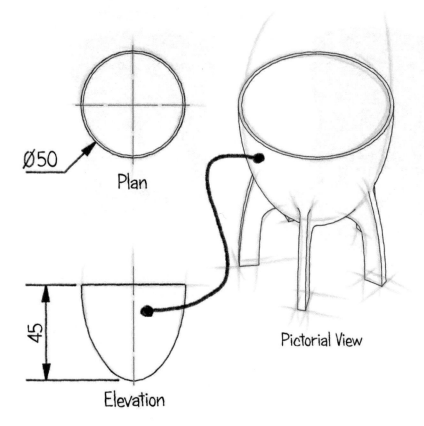

Ø50

Plan

45

Elevation

Pictorial View

The CAD technician used the **revolve** command to model the egg cup body.

(a) Describe, **using the correct dimensions and 3D CAD modelling terms,** how you would use 3D CAD software to model the egg cup body. You may use sketches to support your answer.   3

_____

_____

_____

MARKS | DO NOT WRITE IN THIS MARGIN

2. (continued)

A complete egg cup, a sectioned egg cup and the CAD modelling tree are shown below.

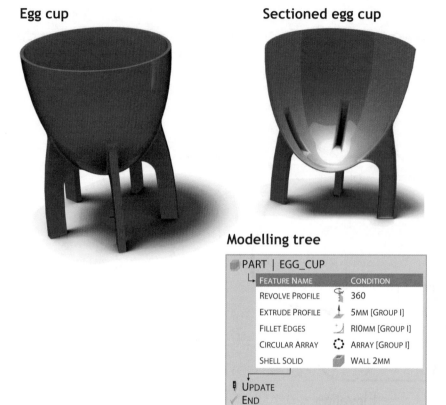

Egg cup

Sectioned egg cup

Modelling tree

PART	EGG_CUP	
FEATURE NAME		CONDITION
REVOLVE PROFILE		360
EXTRUDE PROFILE		5MM [GROUP I]
FILLET EDGES		R10MM [GROUP I]
CIRCULAR ARRAY		ARRAY [GROUP I]
SHELL SOLID		WALL 2MM

UPDATE
END

The first egg cup model was rejected as the legs were hollowed, and this could allow food to become trapped if the egg cup was manufactured.

(b) State how this error could be corrected.   **1**

_____

Total marks   4

3. Production drawings for a new shelf unit, the 'GEO' shelf, are shown below.

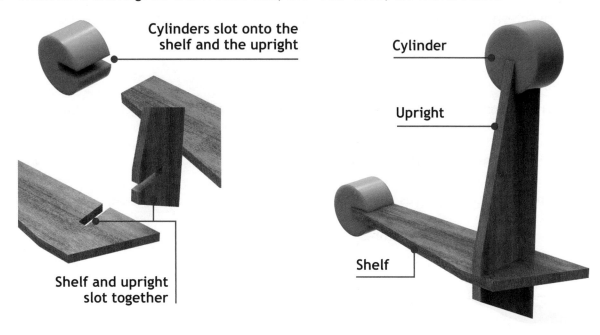

Cylinders slot onto the shelf and the upright

Shelf and upright slot together

Cylinder

Upright

Shelf

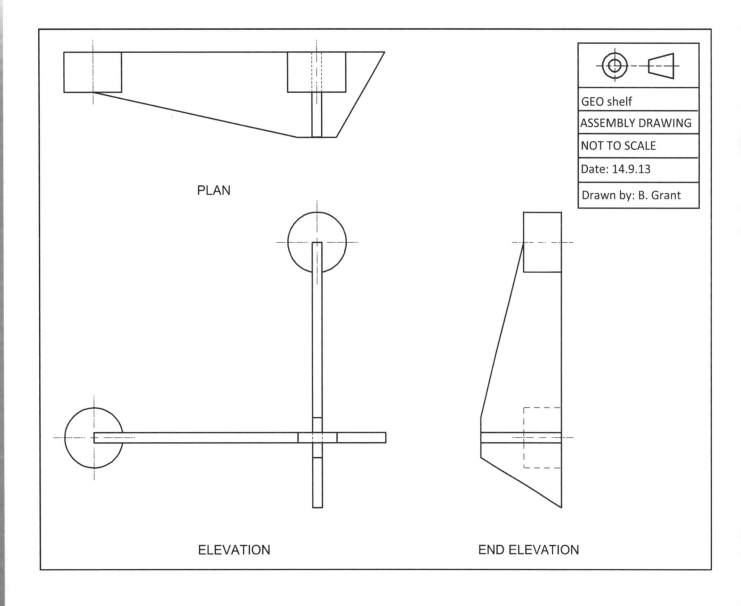

PLAN

ELEVATION

END ELEVATION

GEO shelf

ASSEMBLY DRAWING

NOT TO SCALE

Date: 14.9.13

Drawn by: B. Grant

MARKS | DO NOT WRITE IN THIS MARGIN

3. **(continued)**

The drawings of the cylinder are to be dimensioned so that they can be manufactured.

Measure the orthographic drawings below.

(a) Dimension the views of the cylinder fully and to scale to enable manufacture.   **4**

Apply British Standards conventions correctly.   **4**

Other important features are missing from the drawings of the cylinder.

(b) Add the missing features to the views below. Apply British drawing standards correctly.   **1**

ELEVATION   END ELEVATION

CYLINDER DRAWING	CLIENT - GEO SHELVES	ALL SIZES IN mm	SCALE 1:2	

MARKS | DO NOT WRITE IN THIS MARGIN

3. **(continued)**

An exploded pictorial view of the shelf assembly is shown below.

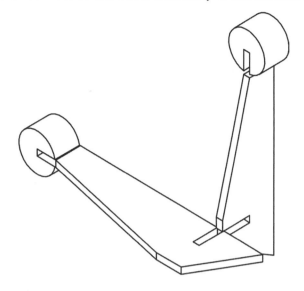

(c) Explain how the clarity of this exploded view can be improved.

1

_____

The pictorial views of components show six designs for shelves and uprights.

Pictorial component views (a–f)

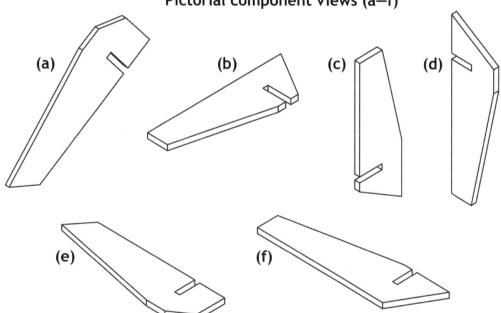

(a) (b) (c) (d)

(e) (f)

(d) State which two of the pictorial component views represent the shelf and the upright used in the 'GEO' shelf unit.

The **shelf** is pictorial component letter _____.

1

The **upright** is pictorial component letter _____.

1

MARKS

3.   (continued)

Pictorial assembly drawing

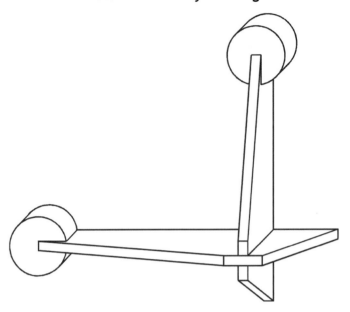

The **pictorial assembly drawing** shown above is a common type of pictorial view.

(e)   Identify the type of pictorial assembly drawing shown.   1

_____

The drawing, view X, shown on the opposite page, is incomplete.

(f)   Complete the drawing, view X, by adding the missing features and applying British Standards conventions. You may sketch or draw your answer directly onto view X or you may annotate the view to describe your answer. Do not include hidden detail.   3

(g)   Add the **correct** view title under the drawing, view X.   1

Total marks 17

3.   (continued)

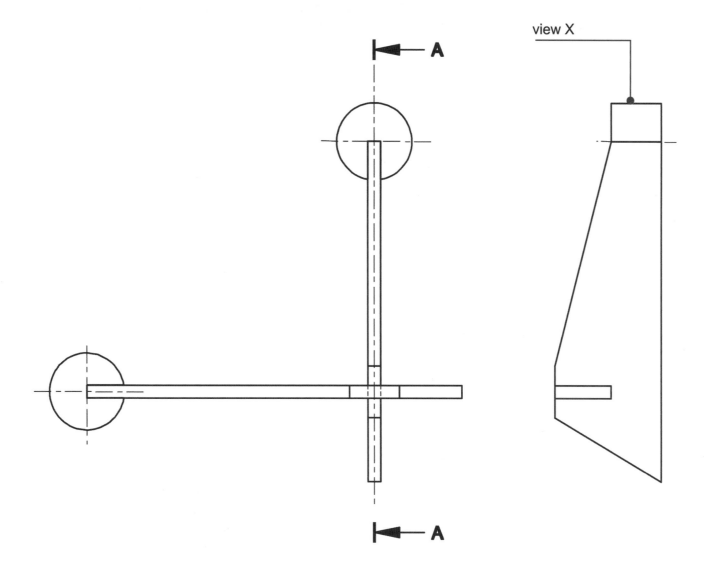

ELEVATION

MARKS | DO NOT WRITE IN THIS MARGIN

4. An architect has chosen to begin a new project by sketching design proposals in a pictorial format. The architect will present these pictorial sketches to the client and discuss their needs.

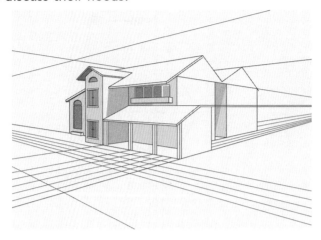

The architect has created a 2-point perspective preliminary sketch to discuss with the client.

(a) Describe why this form of pictorial graphic is suitable for this purpose.   **1**

_____

_____

An architect is considering moving from manual drawing equipment to CAD.

The architect investigated the option and has chosen to stay with manual equipment rather than change to CAD.

(b) Describe two reasons why the architect may have chosen to stay with manual equipment.   **2**

_____

_____

_____

MARKS DO NOT WRITE IN THIS MARGIN

4.   (continued)

The architect will create a range of drawing types, including floor plans and site plans.

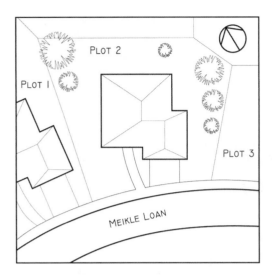

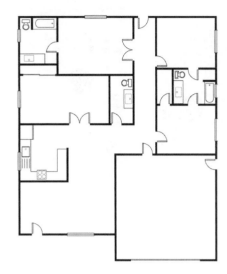

(c)   State the scale most suitable to each plan.

Site Plan scale:_____   1

Floor Plan scale:_____   1

Total marks   5

MARKS | DO NOT WRITE IN THIS MARGIN

5. An environmental charity wants to encourage people to recycle old batteries. They employed a design engineer to make a 'Battery Bin' where people could drop used batteries.

PLAN

END ELEVATION   **ELEVATION**

The graphic designer used 3D CAD to make a 3D model.

(a) Describe, **using 3D CAD modelling terms**, how the CAD model was created. You may use sketches to illustrate your answer.   4

_____

_____

_____

_____

5. (continued)

2D CAD drawings will be produced to enable CNC manufacture. The 'Battery Bin' will be formed from sheet metal. A surface development is required to be marked onto the metal.

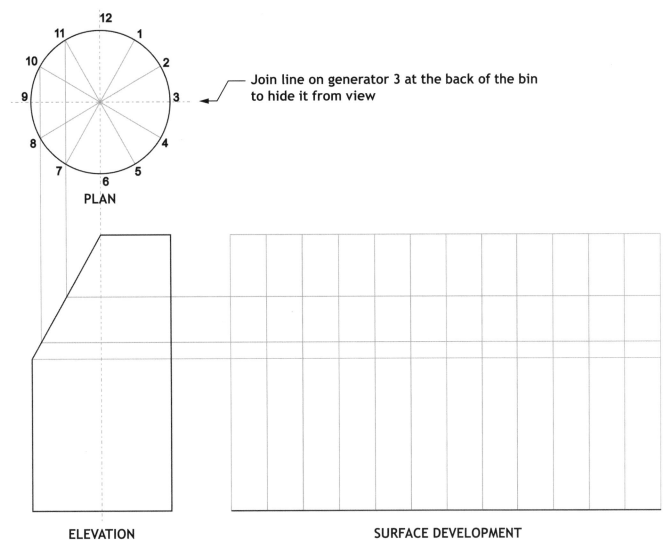

— Join line on generator 3 at the back of the bin to hide it from view

PLAN

ELEVATION   SURFACE DEVELOPMENT

	MARKS	DO NOT WRITE IN THIS MARGIN

(b) Complete the generators by adding numbers to the surface development.   1

(c) Complete the surface development by marking the sloping surface on the generators and adding the outlines. You may sketch your answer or mark crosses on the generators and annotate to describe your answer.   3

5.   (continued)

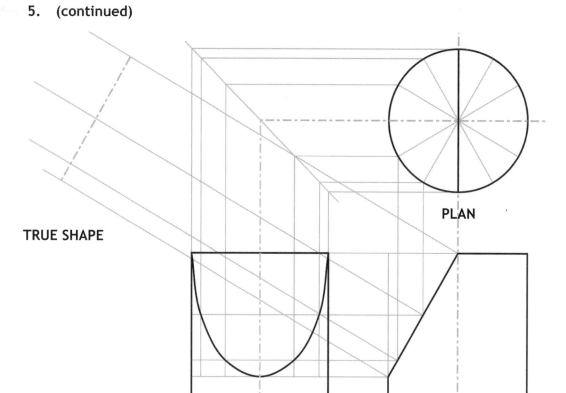

TRUE SHAPE

PLAN

END ELEVATION   ELEVATION

A graphic designer has been employed to design a graphic for the top of the 'Battery Bin'. The graphic designer has requested the **true shape** of the front of the bin.

MARKS | DO NOT WRITE IN THIS MARGIN

5. (continued)

(d) Identify the correct true shape by ticking a box below. **1**

True shape options

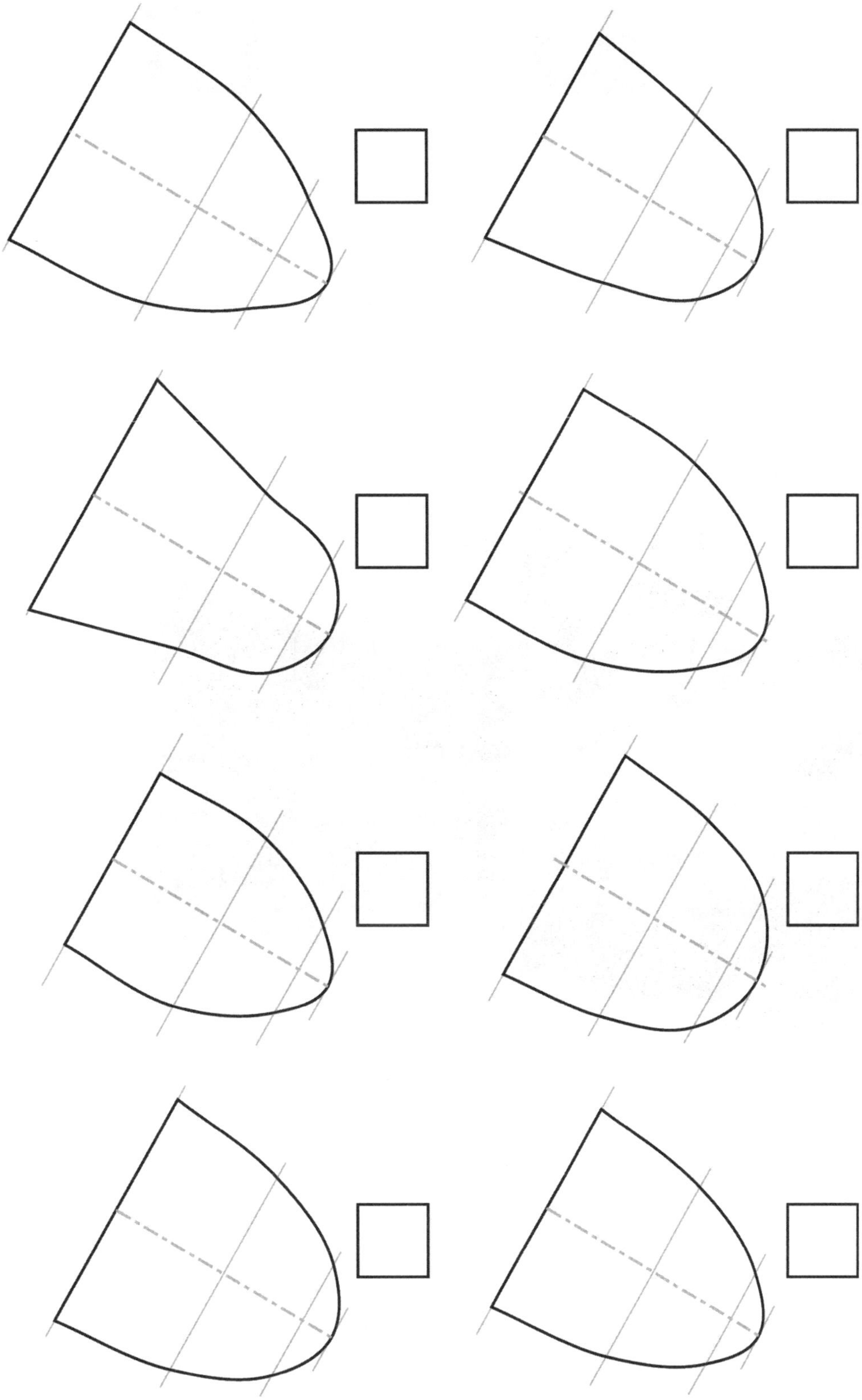

Total marks 9

MARKS | DO NOT WRITE IN THIS MARGIN

6. The following public information signs have all been used in an international airport where travellers are often in a hurry.

(a) State two reasons why graphic symbols, rather than textual information, are used in an international airport.

Reason 1 _____   1

_____

Reason 2 _____   1

_____

The colours chosen for the cafe seating area in the airport are mostly greens and neutral colours with some orange furniture providing the accent colour.

(b) Describe one way in which this colour scheme might benefit travellers.   1

_____

_____

(c) Describe one way in which the colour scheme might support the identity of the airport.   1

_____

_____

Total marks   4

MARKS | DO NOT WRITE IN THIS MARGIN

7. A takeaway company is launching a new range of healthier burgers.

A packaging designer made a preliminary sketch of half of the packaging, shown below. The packaging will be made from two identical hexagonal pyramids.

The company employed a CAD technician to create a 3D model of their new burger box. The first and final steps are shown below.

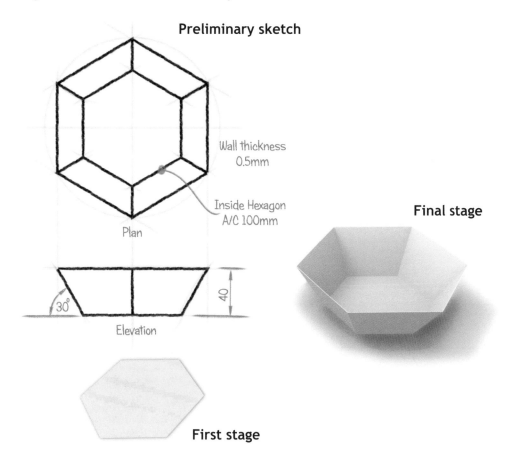

Preliminary sketch

Wall thickness 0.5mm

Inside Hexagon A/C 100mm

Plan

30°

40

Elevation

Final stage

First stage

(a) Describe, with reference to the **sizes in the preliminary sketch**, the modelling techniques used to model this half of the burger box. You may use sketches to illustrate your answer.   **3**

_____

_____

_____

MARKS | DO NOT WRITE IN THIS MARGIN

7. (continued)

The CAD technician used 2D CAD to make the orthographic drawing and the surface development.

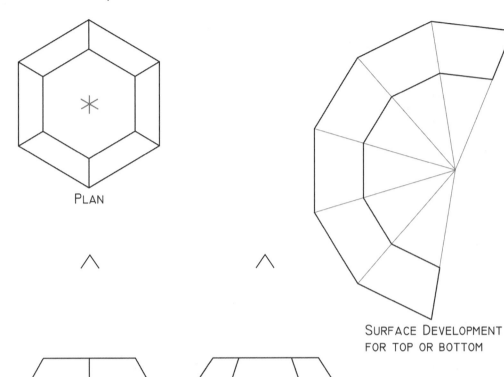

PLAN

SURFACE DEVELOPMENT
FOR TOP OR BOTTOM

ELEVATION   END ELEVATION

True length is used to generate a surface development.

(b) Identify, on the drawing above, where the true length is measured from.   **1**

The surface development requires fold lines.

(c) Identify the correct line type for a fold by ticking a box below.   **1**

- - - - - - - - - - - ☐   — - — - — - — - — ☐

—— - - —— - - —— ☐   · · · · · · · · · · · · · · · ☐

· ☐   - - - - - - - - - - - ☐

MARKS | DO NOT WRITE IN THIS MARGIN

7.   (continued)

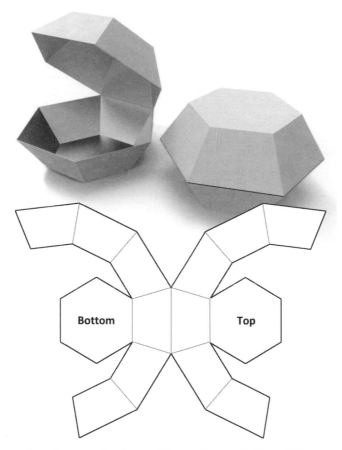

Surface development viewed from the outside of the packaging

Areas of textual information need to be added to the packaging, as indicated in the drawing below:

- Product name
- Sale-by-date
- Nutrition information

(d) Identify, on the surface development above, where the key information must go.

3

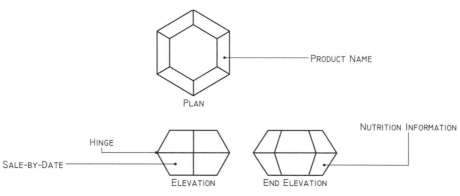

Total marks   8

[END OF MODEL PRACTICE PAPER]

NATIONAL 5

2014

N5

National Qualifications 2014

Mark

X735/75/01

Graphic Communication

THURSDAY, 8 MAY

1:00 PM – 2:30 PM

Fill in these boxes and read what is printed below.

Full name of centre

Town

Forename(s)

Surname

Number of seat

Date of birth

Day	Month	Year
D D	M M	Y Y

Scottish candidate number

Total marks — 60

Attempt ALL questions.

Write your answers clearly in the spaces provided in this booklet. Additional space for answers is provided at the end of this booklet. If you use this space you must clearly identify the question number you are attempting.

All dimensions are in mm.

All technical sketches and drawings use third angle projection.

You may use rulers, compasses or trammels for measuring.

Use **blue** or **black** ink.

Before leaving the examination room you must give this booklet to the Invigilator; if you do not, you may lose all the marks for this paper.

✕SQA

MARKS

1. A graphic designer for a football magazine is commissioned to design a chart or graph. It should display the information in the table below in a visually stimulating and easy to read manner.

English Premier League players' average annual basic wages from 2000–2010	
Season	*Average annual basic wage*
2000–2001	£451,274
2001–2002	£566,932
2002–2003	£611,068
2003–2004	£651,222
2004–2005	£630,355
2005–2006	£685,748
2006–2007	£778,103
2007–2008	£960,377
2008–2009	£1,066,391
2009–2010	£1,162,350

(a) State the most suitable type of chart or graph to use when presenting the information in the table above.　　1

_____

(b) Explain **one** reason for using this type of chart or graph.　　1

_____

_____

Total marks　2

MARKS | DO NOT WRITE IN THIS MARGIN

2. An advertising company has produced a promotional graphic to be used at a sports stadium. The graphic will be placed on the advertising boards around the pitch.

The initial layout is shown below.

Layout 1

(a) State **one** instance where **harmony** has been used in **layout 1**.   1

_____

_____

The graphic artist has decided to change the background colour to violet as shown below.

Layout 2

(b) (i) Explain a reason for changing the background colour to violet.   1

_____

_____

(ii) State whether violet is an advancing or receding colour.   1

_____

(iii) Describe the effect the violet background colour has on the watch.   1

_____

_____

MARKS

2. **(continued)**

The graphic artist wants to change the shade of violet used for the background colour as shown below.

Layout 3

(c) Explain how to create a **shade** of violet.

1

_____

_____

(d) Describe **two** examples of **unity** in **layout 3**.

2

Method 1 _____

_____

Method 2 _____

_____

(e) Describe how the desktop publishing technique '**bleed**' has been used in **layout 3**.

1

_____

_____

(f) Describe how the desktop publishing technique '**reverse**' has been used in **layout 3**.

1

_____

_____

MARKS | DO NOT WRITE IN THIS MARGIN

2. (continued)

The owners of the sports stadium decide to show the advert on their electronic advertising boards.

(g) State **two** environmental benefits of advertising this way. **2**

Benefit 1 ____

Benefit 2 ____

Total marks 11

[Turn over

MARKS

3. Two stages in the production of a 3D CAD model of a headphone connector are shown below.

Stage 1

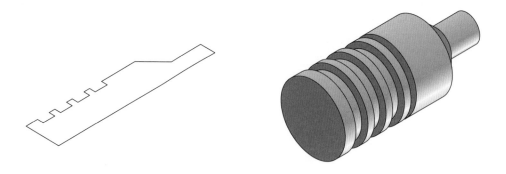

Before   After

Stage 2

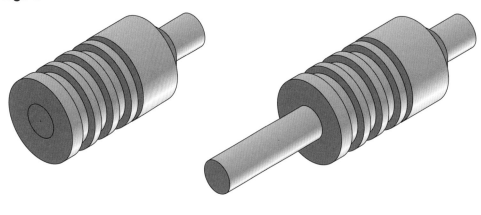

Before   After

(a) State the name of the 3D modelling feature which has been used in Stage 1.

1

_____

(b) State the name of the 3D modelling feature which has been used in Stage 2.

1

_____

Total marks   2

MARKS | DO NOT WRITE IN THIS MARGIN

4. Two building symbols which are commonly found in sectional views of buildings are shown below.

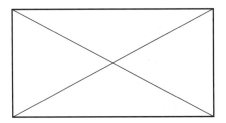

Symbol 1　　　　　　　　**Symbol 2**

State the name of:　　　　　　　　2

Symbol 1 _____

Symbol 2 _____

5. A 3D CAD model of a new craft knife design is shown below.

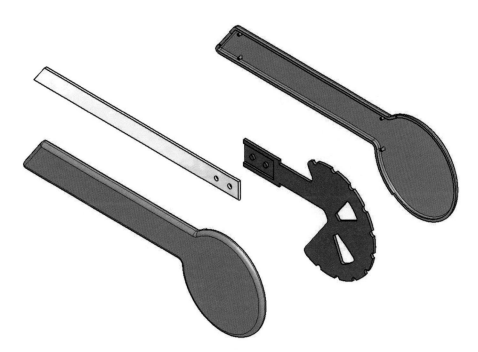

State **three** disadvantages to a design company of using 3D CAD modelling instead of traditional manual modelling.　　　3

1 _____

2 _____

3 _____

6. A variety of views of a child's wooden toy train are shown below.

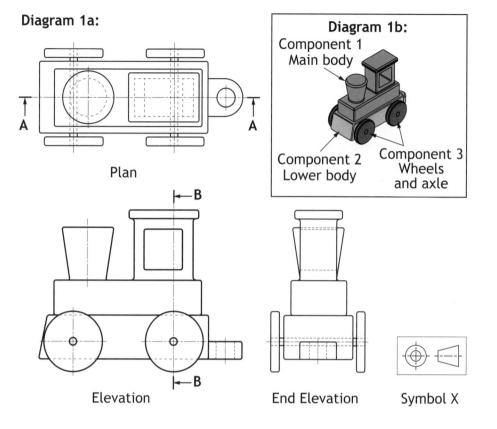

Diagram 1a:

Plan

Diagram 1b:
Component 1
Main body
Component 2
Lower body
Component 3
Wheels
and axle

Elevation

End Elevation

Symbol X

(a) State the name of the type of drawing shown in Diagram 1a.   1

_____

(b) State the name of Symbol X in Diagram 1a.   1

_____

(c) Describe the purpose of Symbol X.   1

_____

6. **(continued)**

Four potential Sectional Elevations of the toy train views are shown below.

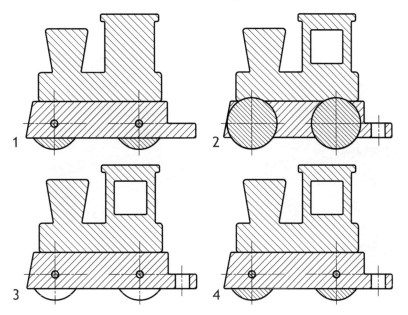

Diagram 2: Sectional Elevations on A—A

(d) State, with reference to Diagram 1a and Diagram 2, the correct Sectional Elevation on A—A.

1

Four potential Sectional End Elevations of the toy train views are shown below

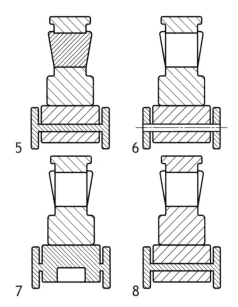

Diagram 3: Sectional End Elevations on B—B

(e) State, with reference to Diagram 1a and Diagram 3, the correct Sectional End Elevation on B—B.

1

MARKS | DO NOT WRITE IN THIS MARGIN

6. (continued)

Two pictorial views of the toy train are shown below.

View 1   **View 2**

(f) State the name of the pictorial view shown at:

    (i) View 1   **1**

_____

    (ii) View 2   **1**

_____

(g) State the name of another **two** types of pictorial views which would be suitable to show the train.   **2**

Pictorial type 1

_____

Pictorial type 2

_____

6.   (continued)

A partial End Elevation complete with relevant dimensions (Diagram 4a) of the toy train is shown below. An End Elevation of the train track is shown (Diagram 4b).

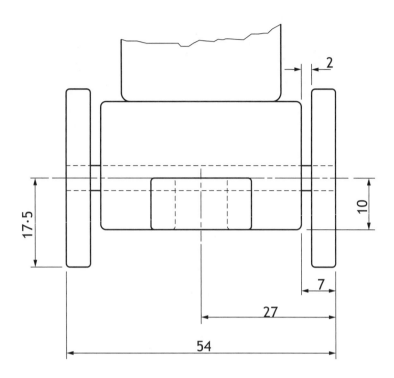

Diagram 4a: Dimensioned Partial End Elevation of the toy train

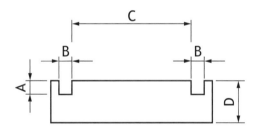

Track End Elevation

Diagram 4b: End Elevation of train track

(h)   State, with reference to Diagram 4a and 4b, a dimension for:

(i)   **A** _____   1

(ii) **B** _____   1

(iii) **C** _____   1

(iv) **D** _____   1

6. (continued)

The train track can be made up with the four different track tiles shown in Diagram 5.

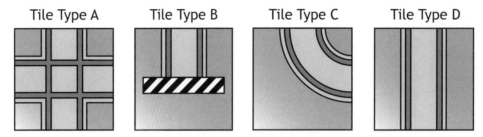

Tile Type A   Tile Type B   Tile Type C   Tile Type D

Diagram 5: Example Track Tiles

Diagram 6 shows a completed track layout using a minimum number of tiles.

Number of type A tiles: 0

Number of type B tiles: 0

Number of type C tiles: 1

Number of type D tiles: 3

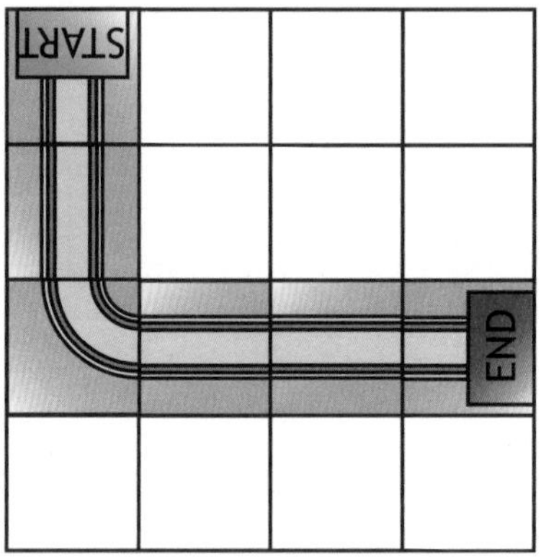

Diagram 6: Completed Track Layout

MARKS

6.   (continued)

Three incomplete track designs are shown below.

(i)   State, with reference to Diagrams 5 and 6, the minimum number of each type of track tile required for each track design. All open ends must be blocked off.

Tiles may be rotated.

(i)   Track design 1:   4

Number of type A tiles:

Number of type B tiles:

Number of type C tiles:

Number of type D tiles:

(ii)   Track design 2:   4

Number of type A tiles:

Number of type B tiles:

Number of type C tiles:

Number of type D tiles:

(iii)   Track design 3 (your track must reach both END points):   4

Number of type A tiles:

Number of type B tiles:

Number of type C tiles:

Number of type D tiles:

Total marks 25

[Turn over

7.   A door handle and door plate were designed using 3D modelling software.

An exploded isometric view of the door handle and door plate is shown below.

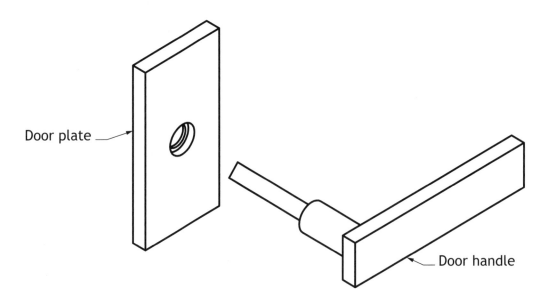

A preliminary orthographic sketch of the door handle (not to scale) is shown below.

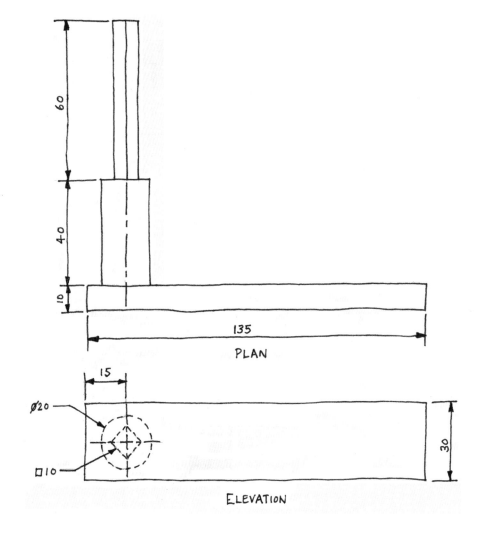

MARKS | DO NOT WRITE IN THIS MARGIN

7. **(continued)**

A Ø20 circle is sketched before the extrude command is used to create step 1.

(a) State the length of the extrusion used in step 1.

1

_____

(b) Describe, with reference to correct dimensions and 3D CAD modelling terms, how you would complete step 2 and step 3.

You may use sketches to support your answer.   4

7. **(continued)**

The door plate is needed to secure the handle to the door. The production orthographic drawing (not to scale) for the door plate is shown below.

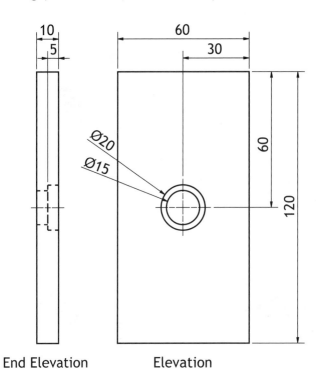

End Elevation   Elevation

(c) Describe, with reference to correct dimensions and 3D CAD modelling terms, how you would create the door plate.

You may use sketches to support your answer.   3

MARKS

7.   (continued)

In order to manufacture the door plate, the back of the plate is hollowed out as shown below.

(d)   State the name of the 3D modelling technique used to hollow the door plate.   1

_____

(e)   State **three** advantages of computer aided drawing over manual drawing methods.   3

Advantage 1 _____

Advantage 2 _____

Advantage 3 _____

When producing the door plate the CAD command 'zoom' is used.

(f)   State one way in which the 'zoom' command would be useful.   1

_____

_____

Total marks   13

[Turn over for Question 8 on *Page eighteen*

MARKS

8. Two graphic items A and B are shown below.

(a) Indicate, using a tick (✓), if Graphic Item **A** is:

Preliminary ☐

Promotional ☐

Production ☐

1

Graphic Item **A**

(b) Indicate, using a tick (✓), if Graphic Item **B** is:

Preliminary ☐

Promotional ☐

Production ☐

1

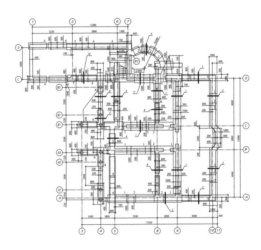

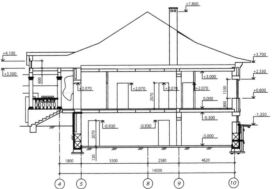

Graphic Item **B**

Total marks   2

[END OF QUESTION PAPER]

ADDITIONAL SPACE FOR ANSWERS

MARKS | DO NOT WRITE IN THIS MARGIN

ADDITIONAL SPACE FOR ANSWERS

NATIONAL 5 GRAPHIC COMMUNICATION SPECIMEN QUESTION PAPER

1. (a)

(i) *Any **one** answer which states clearly where alignment has been used, such as:*
- White text and product name
- Product name and bottle top
- Black line and white text
- Black line and product name
- Black line and bottle top　　　　1

(ii) *Any **one** answer which describes the effect of alignment on Layout 1, for example:*
- It helps organise the layout
- Gives it a structure
- Makes it easier to read/follow
- Helps unify the layout　　　　1

(b) *Any **two** simple descriptions which indicate an understanding of unity, for example:*
- The same colour in the bottle top and green boxes
- Wrapping text around the bottle containing the graphics and text

(One mark per correct description given up to two marks)　　　　2

(c) *Any **two** simple descriptions which indicate an understanding of contrast in the context of Layout 3, for example by:*
- Using green and purple/violet in the layout
- Using vertical and horizontal elements
- Creating depth (near and far)
- Using wavy and straight lines
- Using light and dark tones

(One mark per correct description given up to two marks)　　　　2

(d) *Any **one** logical statement in the context of the question, for example:*
- To create a more usable space to the right
- To make room for text
- To make use of the 'rule of thirds' in the layout
- To create an asymmetric balance
- To create an off-centre focal point　　　　1

(e)

(i) Receding colour　　　　1

(ii) *Any **one** clear description of the effect, for example:*
- It makes the bottle stand out
- It pushes the bottle forward　　　　1

(f) Blue-green
OR
Green-yellow　　　　1

(g) *Any **two** clear statements which show a reduction of impact, such as:*
- Use recycled paper
- Publish online, allowing some of the workforce to work from home
- Use environmentally-friendly inks
- Print in regional offices to minimise carbon footprint of transportation
- Switch off computers

(One mark per correct statement given up to two marks)　　　　2

(h) *Any **one** logical benefit from DTP, for example:*
- Improved speed and accuracy of production
- Images can be easily modified
- Layouts and files can be sent long distances for approval
- Modifications can be made easily and quickly
- DTP users can work from home
- Ease of communication with client　　　　1

2. (a) 50 mm　　　　1

(b) *Any logical description which includes relevant dimensions, for example:*
- Make a sketch on the top face or a work plane parallel to the top and bottom surfaces
- Draw a circle of 30 mm diameter (or 15 mm radius)
- Extrude/protrude/project　　　　3

(c) *Any logical description for a revolved solid OR a double extrusion which includes relevant commands and processes up to four marks.*

As a revolved solid:
Draw a profile similar to below and revolve as long as following criteria are met:
- Pin shaft length must be greater than 90 mm *(1 mark)*
- Candidate must make reference to the pin diameter (<30 mm) *(1 mark)*
- Candidate must make reference to the pin head diameter (>30 mm) *(1 mark)*
- Selecting the centre axis of the profile and revolving *(1 mark)*

As a double extrusion:
- Draw a circle for pin shaft with diameter (<30 mm) *(1 mark)*
- Extrude (>90 mm) *(1 mark)*
- Create a new sketch on a face of the extruded cylinder *(1 mark)*
- Draw a circle diameter (>30 mm) and extrude *(1 mark)*

(Or any similar and appropriate process)　　　　4

(d)

(i) The hidden detail line on the plan view is the wrong line type.

(ii) The cutting plane line type is incorrect.

(iii) The hatch markings on the sectional view are opposing/should be the same.

(One mark per correct answer up to three marks)　　　　3

3. (a)–(f) 2,   4,   6   (cut forms top left to top right)
       7,   14,   11   (cut forms bottom left to bottom right)
       (One mark per correct answer up to six marks)   **6**

4. (a)   (i) Pie chart/pie graph   **1**

   (ii) The data is in percentages/the data represents a whole figure

   Where a candidate has used the incorrect chart type in question **4.** (a) (i) *and the reason they give is appropriate, then a mark should be awarded.*   **1**

   (b)   (i) Line graph or bar chart   **1**

   (ii) **Line graph:** the data has a time component, base or axis/it is important to show the trend or flow of figures
   Bar chart: a comparison between sales in individual months can be shown

   Where a candidate has used the incorrect chart type in question **4.** (b) (i) *and the reason they give is appropriate, then a mark should be awarded.*   **1**

5. (a)   (i)

   1

   (ii) Three windows face east   **1**

   (b)   (i) *Any* **one** *clear statement of an advantage of a CAD library, for example:*
   • Symbols do not have to be re-drawn
   • Saves time
   • Standard symbols for all users means consistency
   1

   (ii) *Any* **one** *clear statement of an advantage of symbols, for example:*
   • Internationally recognised
   • Saves space on drawing
   • Simple to understand   **1**

6. (a) View 5   **1**

   (b) Sectional view 9   **1**

   (c) *Any* **one** *clear explanation of what scale 1:2 means, for example:*
   • Drawn half actual size
   • Actual item is double size of drawing   **1**

   (d) Component or part drawings *(or anything similar)*   **1**

   (e) *Any* **one** *benefit of the use of sectional drawings relating to the door handle, such as:*
   • The manufacturer is able to determine what the inside of the item will look like
   • Helps with manufacturing
   • Helps to understand the components
   • Helps to understand how it assembles/shows how parts go together   **1**

   (f) Third angle projection symbol   **1**

   (g) *Any* **one** *description of the correct purpose of the third angle symbol, for example:*
   • Allows the reader to understand from which direction the views are projected
   • To explain the layout of the drawing or the views   **1**

   (h) *Any* **one** *correct location statement, such as:*
   • In the title block/information bar
   • Block or box   **1**

7. (a) (i–ii)

   (One mark per correct location)   **2**

7. (b)   • Bracket 1–2
   • Bracket 2–4
   • Bracket 3–2
   • Bracket 4–4
   (One mark per correct answer up to four)   **4**

8. (a)   (i) *Any one statement which demonstrates cropping, for example:*
   • Fully cropped
   • Image cut out
   • Irregular crop
   • Cropped   **1**

   (ii) Drop shadow added   **1**

   (iii) *Any one statement which demonstrates an alteration to the font/word, for example:*
   • Change font style
   • Typeface
   • Reverse
   • Tilted
   • Rotated   **1**

   (iv) *Any one edit to the slogan, such as:*
   • Flow text along a path
   • Flow text
   • Reverse   **1**

   (v) Transparency   **1**

   (b) *Any one statement, such as:*
   • Creates the impression of movement
   • Creates rhythm
   • Creates contrast
   • Makes it legible
   • Allows more text to fit the space   **1**

   (c) *Any two statements, such as:*
   • Creates a structure to work on
   • Helps create a structure in the layout
   • Improves accuracy
   • Helps aid alignment
   • Improves speed of production
   (Or similar)   **2**

NATIONAL 5 GRAPHIC COMMUNICATION MODEL PAPER 1

1. (a) Background colours are receding or contrasting and help the red advancing colour to stand out. **1**

(b) Text wrap; wrap text **1**

(c) To separate items; to help create structure; to emphasise the company name **1**

(d) Flow text; flow text along a path **1**

(e) Reverse; reverse text *('Font style' will not be accepted as an answer.)* **1**

(f) Creates contrast with the straight lines in the layout; creates a close connection between the product and the slogan; reflects the sentiment of the text: soft and smooth, suggests comfort or cushioning, suggests movement. **1**

(g) Graded, gradient or gradiation fill **1**

2. (a)

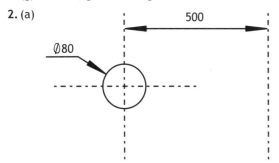

Draw a circle of DIA80mm *(1 mark)*, 500mm away from a centre line. *(1 mark)*

Revolve the circular profile 180° round the centre line. *(1 mark)* **3**

(b) Select the flat face of a slot; draw a mirror line; select a plane. *(1 mark for either of these)* Use the mirror command to mirror the component. **2**

(c)

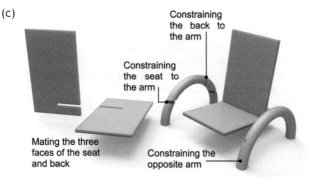

Assemble the chair seat and back requiring three mates. *(1 mark)* Mate the chair to leg/arm base. *(1 mark)* Mate the chair to leg/arm back. *(1 mark)* Constrain opposite arm using same technique. *(1 mark)* **4**

3. (a) and (b)

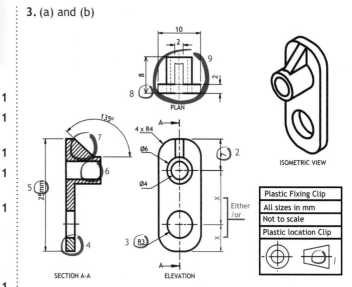

2

Table of British Standards errors and omissions in the fixing clip production drawing	
Your numbered error or omission	**Description of error or omission**
1	This should be a centre line, not a solid line.
2	The number is underneath the dimension line; it should be on top
3	This dimension should be a diameter, not a radius.
4	Cross-hatching is in the wrong direction; one component = one direction
5	Units should not be shown; they appear already in the title block.
6	Centre line is missing.
7	The web is section and should not be.
8	Open arrows on the dimension line; these should be closed.
9	The plan is upside-down.

8

(c) **CAD models** are electronic and can be quickly and easily sent to China via email attachments. **1**

Drawing standards are common around the world and can be understood by all users. Drawing standards help overcome language barriers. **1**

(d) CAD models are easily modified to take account of changes to the design; CAD models can be tested before being manufactured; the CAD model can be used to produce a CNC prototype; CAD models can be rendered to produce a realistic image; CAD models can be tested in computer simulations; production drawings can be easily generated from CAD models. **2**

(e) Exploded pictorial view iii **1**

4. (a) The pale blue colours used in the improved sign are suitable because they are associated with cleanliness and are calming in nature; the two tones used help the user follow the information across the sign. *(Or any other suitable answer)* 2

(b) The sans-serif font used has no formatting (italic, bold, underline) and is clear and easy to read.
OR
The new font is simpler and more modern. It is less formal, less old-fashioned, etc. It is not italicised. *(There is no need to specifically mention serif or sans-serif typefaces.)* 1

(c) The line separating 'Department' and 'Floor' is removed; the department titles are accurately aligned; the floor numbers are 'reduced' on the improved sign; departments are grouped; 'You are here' is clear on the improved sign; the coloured banding makes connecting the department and floor easier. *(Any two points, for one mark each)* 2

5. (a) Isometric exploded view A 1

(b) When the physical hook assembles, the hook will need to be placed on top of the wall bracket from the top. 1

(c)

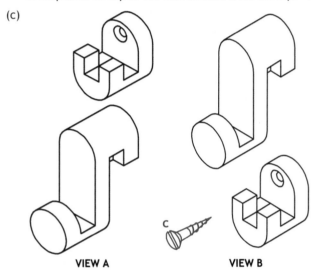

VIEW A　　　　**VIEW B**
1

(d) Section A–A is view S. 1

(e) Section B–B is view Y. 1

(f) Exploded views show how the components in a product fit together; exploded views can help to show the assembler or consumer the best way to assemble a product. 1

(g) Sectional views give an understanding of how parts fit together; sectional views can show the features inside components and assemblies that cannot normally be seen. 1

(h) Webs; shafts; spindles; axles; nuts and bolts. *(Any one)* 1

(i) An assembly drawing is a drawing of a product that has more than one part and the parts are put together as they will be in the real product. Component drawings are drawings of individual parts. 1

(j) Component drawings are dimensioned prior to manufacture because each part is normally manufactured separately and assembled later. Dimensioning assembly drawings would be confusing because it may not be clear which component the dimensions apply to. 1

6. (a) Line graph
OR
Bar graph 1

(b) The line graph has a time base and is the best choice to show a flow or trend over a period of time.
OR
The bar graph will give a comparison between sales in different months. 1

(c) A table 1

(d) The data is too complex to present using any of the other types of information graphic. 1

7. (a) North arrow; scale of drawing; room names; dimensions; ceiling lights; electrical sockets; wall switches. *(Any three)* 3

(b) ▬▬▬▬▬▬▬▬▬▬▬▬

(Symbol added in a suitable position to any room.)

8. (a) Matching the colour of green in two items; the red flashbar is layered behind the title and the young people and the student ID card which physically connects them all; the phone number is in very close proximity to the image of young people. *(Any one)* 1

(b) By layering items on top of other items; ID card over flashbar; young people over the flashbar; etc. *(Any one)* 1

(c) Alignment occurs between the title and the ID card; the right end of the title and the right edge of the phone number are aligned; the flow text is carefully aligned to the ID card. *(Any one)* 1

(d) Depth by layering (near and far); size (big and small text, people, etc.); vertical and horizontal; straight and curved (wavy). *(Any one)* 1

(e) Contrast can make the layout eye-catching. This is important to attract attention or when the poster is moving along a roadside and has a brief viewing time. 1

(f) The most dominant item is: group of young people OR the title OR the ID card.
The designer created dominance by: the image of young people is on the top layer, at the front, they are in close up (large) OR title is on a red (advancing) background and so stands out well OR ID card is layered on top of the title and the curved shape gives it dominance. *(Any one pair)* 1

NATIONAL 5 GRAPHIC COMMUNICATION MODEL PAPER 2

1. (a)

	DTP edit
The L-COM product name	rotate/flip
The slogan ('A NEW DAWN …' etc.)	flow text along a path
The body text	left aligned or text wrap
The image of the L-COM product	drop shadow

4

(b) Layering and overlapping images on top of other images creates a physical connection; using an accent colour (red or blue) in more than one area creates a unity through colour; text wrap creates a connection between the body text and the product. *(Any two)* **2**

(c) The product is pictorial and creates a strong 3D image; the product is in perspective and has a near corner and a far corner; the product is on the top layer; the drop shadow creates depth and emphasis. *(Any two)* **2**

(d) Vertical colour fill and horizontal line; near and far; 2D shapes and a 3D image; large and small text. *(Any two)* **2**

(e) Asymmetric balance **1**

(f) It creates depth by passing behind the product image; it helps create asymmetric balance; it creates contrast with the blue colour fill; it creates unity with the red button; it creates strong alignment with the header and footer. *(Any one)* **1**

(g) Space at the top   Header space
Space at the bottom   Footer space **2**

(h) Reverse text (*'Reverse' will be accepted*) **1**

2. (a) Draw a construction line horizontally through the incomplete profile. (In the middle – 60 mm from top and bottom). *(1 mark)*
Select the rectangular slot and use the mirror tool to mirror the rectangle about the centre. *(1 mark)* **2**

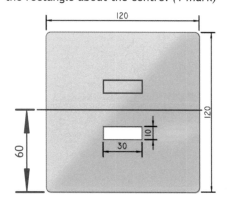

(b)

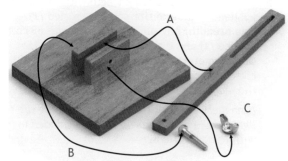

Centre axis to the upright, nut and bolt to the base.
Mate the flat face of upright to inside of base (A to A as shown above).
Mate the flat face of bolt to outside of base (B to B as shown above).
Mate the flat face of the nut to outside of base (C to C as shown above). **4**

(c) Standard components are pre-drawn and can be assembled directly – this saves time. They are drawn to the particular standards of common component parts and can be modified as the design develops and changes. **2**

(d) Exploded isometric view. **1**

(e) Customers can see easily see how the lamp assembles; customers do not need to understand complex orthographic drawings; customers may find it easier to follow a drawing rather than a written description. *(Any one)* **1**

(f) The lighting effect can be simulated; the range of motion can be tested; the strength of materials can be tested. *(Any two)* **2**

3. (a)

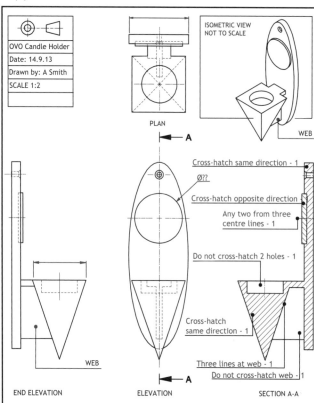

7

(b) **One length:** Any suitable length with BS correctly applied *(1)* and the size correctly scaled *(1)*.
One breadth: Any suitable breadth with BS correctly applied *(1)* and the size correctly scaled *(1)*.
One diameter: Any suitable diameter with BS correctly applied *(1)* and the size correctly scaled *(1)*.
(No marks awarded for dimensioning height.) **6**

(d) *(One mark each for showing or describing the tea-light candle and mirror in 2D and exploded in line with their locations.)*

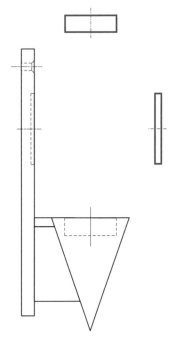

EXPLODED END ELEVATION

2

4. (a) Advancing colour **1**

(b) It makes the title stand out more; it throws it forward; it creates contrast with the other main colours in the layout. *(Any one)* **1**

(c) The (neutral brown) colours should appeal to the older target market; the browns suggest natural materials; the colours represent wood craft (the hobby of the customer); the colours give the advert a more traditional look which is suitable for an older target market. *(Any one)* **1**

(d) **Advert 1:** The font is a fun style that will appeal to young children and their young parents; it supports (matches) the fun theme promoted through the toys. *(Any one)* **1**
Advert 2: The font is a more traditional, formal or old fashioned style that will appeal to the older target market (do not need to mention serif/sans-serif font); the font is more formal and likely to appeal to an older target market which likes traditional crafts. *(Any one)* **1**

(e) **Advantage:** It reduces paper costs; it is environmentally friendly (no paper production); it creates a more personal or direct contact with potential customers; it is immediate (quick) and can happen whenever the company likes without waiting for a magazine to come out. *(Any one or any other suitable answer)* **1**
Disadvantage: It may limit mass contact with potential customers; it may impact on the employment opportunities in paper publishing and production; it will require a large database. *(Any one or any other suitable answer)* **1**

5. (a) It is quicker/easier to modify a CAD model; CAD models can be used to create a surface development; CAD models can be illustrated to look like metal; CAD models can be illustrated in a range of scenes; it is easier to store a CAD file than a physical model. *(Any two)* **2**

(b) A/C means 'across corners'. It refers to the size of the hexagon on the display stand. **2**

(c) To aid manufacture; to aid production drawings with sizes; to add dimensions; to aid the DTP for the true shape on top; to understand the proportions of the stand from each elevation. *(Any two)* **2**

(d)

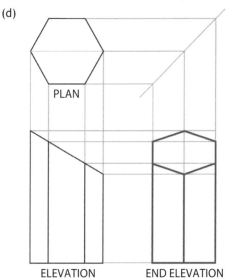

PLAN

ELEVATION   END ELEVATION

4

(e)

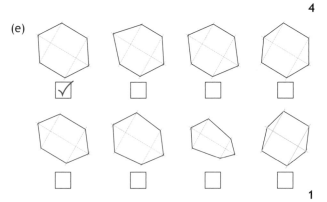

1

NATIONAL 5 GRAPHIC COMMUNICATION MODEL PAPER 3

1. (a) Transparency 1

  (b) Text wrap 1

  (c) Fully cropped

    OR

    Fully masked 1

  (d) It allows a new background to be introduced; allows layering; creates a shape to contrast with rectangles; emphasises the figure; allows the old background to be removed. *(Any one)* 1

  (e) Font style; reverse

    OR

    Font colour; drop shadow. *(Any one)* 1

  (f) Footer space 1

  (g) The product name, the slogan and the web address are all carefully aligned down the left hand edge. ... 1

  (h) Alignment helps bring a neatness, structure or organised look to the layout. 1

  (i) The colour fill (flashbar) connects the background, the product, product name and the jogger; the blue line connects the product and the figure; the text wrap connects the slogan to the figure; the red colour matching connects the product with the colour fill; blue is used in the background, the jogger and the line, connecting them visually; overlapping (layering) physically connects items that touch. *(Any two)* ... 2

  (j) Layering and overlapping images create depth; drop shadows behind the jogger and product name create depth. *(Any one)* 1

  (k) The bottle is larger in scale than other items; is on the top layer; is positioned close to a (rule of thirds) focal point. *(Any one)* 1

  (l) The colour of the bottle was selected with the colour picker and the colour fill was created in exactly the same colour. 1

2. (a)

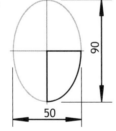

Draw an ellipse with a major axis of 90 mm and minor axis of 50 mm. Trim the ellipse to leave ¼.	Revolve the profile 360°.	Select the top face and shell the solid to 2 mm.

    3

  (b) The shell solid command is in the wrong position in the modelling tree. Move it to just after the revolve profile. 1

3. (a) Marks awarded for showing or describing the four vital (scaled up) dimensions *(for 1 mark each)*. *(Apply a 1mm tolerance throughout.)* Vital dimensions added without being scaled *(2 marks only)*. Each dimension must be described or shown **correctly** to British Standards *(for 1 mark each)*.

    (Dimension layout and style may differ from marking scheme but must conform to British Standards.) ... **4**

  (b) *(Three centre lines correctly applied or described. All three required for 1 mark.)* 1

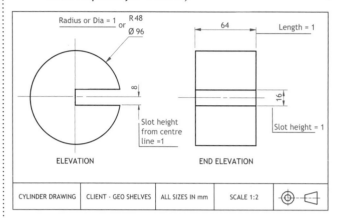

  (c) The components are not separated enough; create clear space between each component in the exploded view. 1

  (d) The **shelf** is pictorial component letter _d_. 1

    The **upright** is pictorial component letter _b_. 1

  (e) Oblique view 1

  (f) *(Cross hatching added or described and with direction changes and staggering. 1 mark for each section.)* ... 3

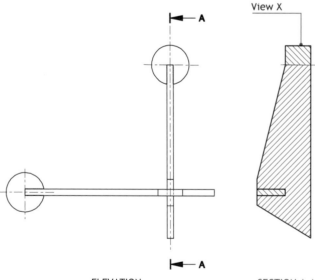

  (g) 'Section A–A' as shown above. 1

4. (a) Perspective graphics are more realistic and show proportion, with items further away getting smaller; a perspective drawing is easily understood by people without a technical background. *(Any one)* 1

  (b) The cost of retraining may be large; the high cost of purchasing CAD equipment and software; manual drawing equipment is already available. *(Any two)* ... 2

  (c) Site plan <u>1:200</u> 1

    Floor plan <u>1:50</u> 1

5. (a) Draw a circle on the base workplane and extrude as a cylinder.
Draw a subtracting shape on the frontal workplane and subtract it to make the slope.
Make the cylinder hollow by using the shell command.
Extrude a circular sketch on the sloping face to make a hole. **4**

(b) and (c)

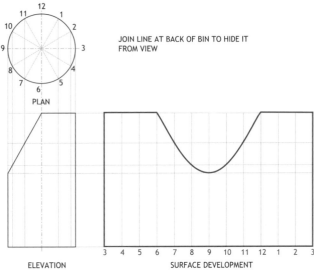

JOIN LINE AT BACK OF BIN TO HIDE IT FROM VIEW

1 and 3

(d)

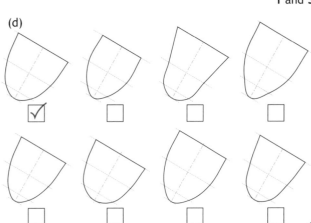

1

6. (a) **Reason 1:** Symbols overcome language barriers. **1**
Reason 2: Symbols are quicker to interpret than text. **1**

(b) Orange creates a refreshing contrast with green; green is a fresh and natural colour, both of which are important in a cafe or restaurant *(would also accept that orange is an appetite colour)*; green is a relaxing colour, important in a hectic airport. *(Any one)* **1**

(c) A common colour scheme creates a unified identity or impression; orange creates contrast with green and is, in this instance, a unifying accent colour. *(Any one)* **1**

7. (a) Extrude the hexagon 40 mm with a taper angle of 30°. Shell the solid 0.5 mm. **3**

(b)

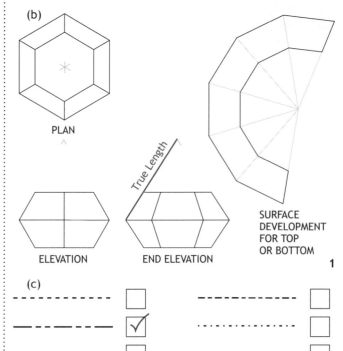

PLAN

True Length

ELEVATION   END ELEVATION

SURFACE DEVELOPMENT FOR TOP OR BOTTOM

1

(c)

1

(d)

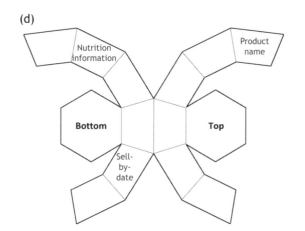

Surface development viewed from the outside of the packaging

3

NATIONAL 5 GRAPHIC COMMUNICATION 2014

1. (a) Line graph is the most suitable

   (b) • Shows the steady growth over a specific period of time
   • Shows trend easily
   • No large differences between items on the "y" axis

2. (a) Green background and yellow watch

   (b) (i) • Violet/purple looks more classy and luxurious
   • To create contrast with the yellow watch
   • To create contrast
   • To make the watch more eye catching

   (ii) Receding

   (iii) • Emphasises the yellow watch
   • Makes the yellow watch stand out more
   • To make the watch more eye catching

   (c) Add black or grey

   (d) • Yellow text 'UTZ' and yellow watch (or any yellow feature of the watch)
   • White circles/bubbles and white divisions on the watch face and white text.
   • Shape of watch face, bubbles and full stops.

   (e) The watch/image/graphic runs into the margin space and/or off the edge of the advert

   Image overlaps the side/edge of the advert/page.

   (f) • White text on violet background
   • Text changed to white

   (g) • No printing so less ink/toner
   • No printing paper
   • No transportation as advert can be emailed to the stadium.

3. (a) Revolution/Revolved solid/Revolve

   (b) Extrusion/Extrude

4. Symbol 1 – Sawn Timber
   Symbol 2 – Concrete

5. • Start-up costs
   • Staff training on new software/ technology
   • Cost to regularly update software
   • Costs for maintenance of equipment
   • Potential loss of work/files through system crashes
   • Easy theft of data/hacking
   • Ergonomic testing cannot take place

6. (a) Orthographic

   (b) Third angle projection/Third angle

   (c) • To show the way the views are projected/laid out
   • To show projection type used
   • Orientation/layout of views

   (d) View 3

   (e) View 6

   (f) (i) Isometric view

   (ii) 2 point perspective view

   (g) Oblique/1 point perspective/ planometric

(h) (i) 7.5mm

   (ii) 5mm

   (iii) 44mm

   (iv) Response must be larger than 7.5mm

(i) Some answers will have two combinations see below:

   (i) tileA= 0   0
   tileB= 0 or 0
   tileC= 2   4
   tileD= 3   1

   (ii) tileA= 0
   tileB= 0
   tileC= 1
   tileD= 2

   (iii) tileA= 1   1
   tileB= 1 or 1
   tileC= 4   3
   tileD= 1   2

7. (a) 40mm

   (b) **Step 2**
   • On one end of the cylinder sketch/draw a rectangle 135mm × 30mm
   • Extrude the rectangle 10mm

   Step 3
   • On the other end of the cylinder sketch/draw a 10mm × 10mm square in the centre
   • Extrude the square 60mm

   Or any similar and appropriate process

   (c) • Sketch a rectangle 120mm × 60mm and extrude 10mm
   • In the centre of the rectangle draw a circle Ø20mm and extrude subtraction/subtract 5mm.
   • In the centre of the circle above, sketch a circle Ø15mm and extrude as a subtraction/subtract 5mm

   Or any similar and appropriate process

   (d) Shell

   (e) Any of;
   • Library of common parts can be used to reduce time
   • Ease of editing
   • Ease of creating new designs from existing designs
   • Less physical storage space required
   • Portable files easier and quicker to transfer by digital means.
   • Accuracy
   • Ability to use in different scenarios (use as base for 3D models)
   • Used for simulations
   • Simultaneous working

   (f) • Zoom allows the user to focus in on smaller details
   • to get an enlarged view of a small part

8. (a) Promotional

   (b) Production

Acknowledgements

Permission has been sought from all relevant copyright holders and Hodder Gibson is grateful for the use of the following:

Image © Jacek Chabraszewski/Shutterstock.com (SQP page 12);
Image © Sychugina/Shutterstock.com (SQP page 23);
Image © LuckyPhoto/Shutterstock.com (SQP page 23);
Image © Andrey_Popov/Shutterstock.com (SQP page 23);
Image © rvika/Shutterstock.com (SQP page 23);
Image © Ting Hoo/Getty Images/Thinkstock (Model Paper 1 page 2);
Image © Getty Images/iStockphoto/Thinkstock (Model Paper 1 page 2);
Image © bagiuiani – Fotolia (Model Paper 1 page 15);
Image © bagiuiani – Fotolia (Model Paper 1 page 15);
Image © d_arts / Shutterstock.com (Model Paper 1 page 15);
Image © Getty Images/iStockphoto/Thinkstock (Model Paper 1 page 16);
Image © eteimaging – Fotolia (Model Paper 1 page 17);
Image © Edyta Pawlowska /www.123rf.com/photo_15623110 (Model Paper 1 page 17);
Image © Ozerina Anna / Shutterstock.com (Model Paper 2 page 2);
Image © Gouraud Studio – Fotolia (Model Paper 2 page 11);
Image © Harvepino / Shutterstock.com (Model Paper 2 page 11);
Image © smuki – Fotolia (Model Paper 2 page 11);
Image © aleksangel – Fotolia (Model Paper 2 page 11);
Image © coramax – Fotolia (Model Paper 2 page 11);
Image © Tatyana Gladskih – Fotolia (Model Paper 2 page 11);
Image © shooarts – Fotolia (Model Paper 2 page 11);
Image © pilarts – Fotolia (Model Paper 2 page 11);
Image © chamillew – Fotolia (Model Paper 2 page 11);
Image © viperagp – Fotolia (Model Paper 2 page 11);
Image © Stanislav Dobrochaso – Fotolia (Model Paper 2 page 11);
Image © Chlorophylle – Fotolia (Model Paper 2 page 11);
Image © Philip Date / Shutterstock.com (Model Paper 3 page 2);
Image © Edie Layland – Fotolia (Model Paper 3 page 2);
Image © Olga Khoroshunova – Fotolia (Model Paper 3 page 2);
Image © Getty Images/iStockphoto/Thinkstock (Model Paper 3 page 12);
Image © Getty Images/iStockphoto/Thinkstock (Model Paper 3 page 12);
Image © nahariyani100 – Fotolia (Model Paper 3 page 12);
Image © Getty Images/iStockphoto/Thinkstock (Model Paper 3 page 18);
Image © haveseen – Fotolia (Model Paper 3 page 18);
Image © Getty Images/iStockphoto/Thinkstock (Model Paper 3 page 18);
Image © Getty Images/iStockphoto/Thinkstock (Model Paper 3 page 18);
Image © Getty Images/Hemera/Thinkstock (Model Paper 3 page 18);
Image © AlexRoz/Shutterstock.com (2014 pages 3 & 4);
Image © Lena Pan/Shutterstock.com (2014 page 18);
Image © vector photo video/Shutterstock.com (2014 page 18).

Hodder Gibson would like to thank SQA for use of any past exam questions that may have been used in model papers, whether amended or in original form.